# MARY I

# MARY I

## THE HISTORY OF AN UNHAPPY TUDOR QUEEN

*by Winifred Roll*

PRENTICE-HALL, INC.
ENGLEWOOD CLIFFS, NEW JERSEY

B

Mary I

Printed in the United States of America                                    ·J

Prentice-Hall International, Inc., London
Prentice-Hall of Australia, Pty. Ltd., North Sydney
Prentice-Hall of Canada, Ltd., Toronto
Prentice-Hall of India Private Ltd., New Delhi
Prentice-Hall of Japan, Inc., Tokyo
Prentice-Hall of Southeast Asia Pte. Ltd., Singapore

10      9      8      7      6      5      4      3      2      1

Library of Congress Cataloging in Publication Data

Roll, Winifred, Lady.    Mary I : the history of an unhappy Tudor Queen.

  Bibliography: p.    Includes index.    SUMMARY: A biography of the daughter of Henry VIII and Katharine of Aragon who, during a brief reign, tried to bring Protestant England back to the Roman Catholic Church.    1. Mary I, Queen of England, 1516-1558—Juvenile literature. 2. Great Britain—History—Mary I, 1553-1558—Juvenile literature. 3. Great Britain—Kings and rulers—Biography—Juvenile literature. [1. Mary I, Queen of England, 1516-1558. 2. Queens. 3. Great Britain—History—Mary I, 1553-1558] I. Title.
DA347.R62                    942.5'4'0924 [B]                    78-16779
ISBN 0-13-559096-5

*Designed by Ernie Haim*

End paper illustration of the Coronation Procession of Edward VI from the Tower of London to Westminster in 1547. REPRODUCED BY COURTESY OF THE SOCIETY OF ANTIQUARIES OF LONDON.

Frontispiece illustration of Mary I wearing the pendant pearl "La Peregrina" thought to have been sent her by Philip the month before their wedding. (HANS EWORTH. C. 1554) SOCIETY OF ANTIQUARIES, LONDON

# CONTENTS

# PREFACE

Mary Tudor's life was dramatic and sad. Her reputation after her death was that of a bloodthirsty Queen. Early histories of her reign were influenced by the author's religious point of view and it was not until the nineteenth century that attempts were made to see her in her true light. In the following pages I have tried to tell her story without bias and to let the facts speak for themselves. But to write a book of this size when the material available is so vast means that I have had to be selective. Consciously or unconsciously, some personal judgment may well be reflected in the choice of quotations and anecdotes. For instance, in view of present-day attitudes I have deliberately drawn attention to occasions when Mary's competence was questioned only because she was a woman—though this was not unnatural in the sixteenth century. As this is a biography, not a history of the Tudor period, the emphasis may sometimes also be misleading. Henry's later life was not spent thinking out ways to oppress his daughters—or his wives; Somerset had other things to occupy his mind than Mary's intransigence: wars with France and with

Scotland, the Turkish invasion of Europe, relationships with the Emperor and Pope, religious wars on the continent, civil disturbances, inflation and unemployment at home. And because Mary is the chief character, more powerful personalities, such as her father and sister, are subordinated to her less effective one.

Some important events of the period are only mentioned, or omitted altogether. In particular, I have not gone into the history of the Reformation or distinguished between Roman Catholicism, Henrician Catholicism and the different kinds of Protestantism—if, indeed, at this period a strict definition is possible. But for those who would like to know more of these matters relevant books have been included in the reading list.

I have drawn almost entirely from contemporary or near-contemporary sources, especially the English, Spanish and Venetian State Papers. As these were gathered together and some of them translated into English during the nineteenth century, there is sometimes a slightly old-fashioned flavor in the style which I have not changed. All spellings, however, have been modernized, and I have, perhaps arbitrarily, standardized spellings of proper names.

Finally, I would like to thank my family and friends for their interest and patience, Anne Senanayake-van Zeeland for making time in her busy life to type the manuscript, and the staffs of the British Library, the London Library, and the Widener Library at Harvard for their assistance.

# INTRODUCTION

A brief introduction may be of interest to those readers who are not already familiar with the background history or events immediately preceding Mary's reign. It is not included in the main story as most of the ground was covered in *The Pomegranate and The Rose*, my book on the life of Katharine of Aragon.

The Tudor period began in 1485 when the Wars of the Roses, which had ravaged England on and off for over sixty years, ended in a victory for Mary's grandfather, Henry VII. The struggle for power between the descendants of two of the sons of Edward III—the Duke of York (White Rose) and the Duke of Lancaster (Red Rose) was brought to a conclusion by the marriage of Henry Tudor (leader of the Lancastrians) to Elizabeth of York. Their children united both houses and the Tudor emblem was the red and white rose.

There were, however, other Yorkist descendants whose very existence was a threat to the newly consolidated kingdom. To prevent any uprising on their behalf, the leading members of the family were sent to the block—the Earl of Warwick by Henry VII and the Earl of Suffolk by Henry VIII in the early years of his reign. Later, when lack of a royal heir made the remaining Yorkists assume a more menacing aspect as successors to the throne, there were other executions—Margaret Pole, Countess of Salisbury (the Earl of Warwick's sister), and her son Henry, who were also anathema to Henry VIII as past supporters of the cause of Katharine of Aragon. But the Countess of Salisbury's son Reginald and Edward Courtenay survived to play important roles in Mary's day.

An England united meant a stronger England: a country which could better withstand attacks from Scotland, which could take its place in Europe and help maintain the balance of power by strategic alliances. A dynastic marriage was one way of cementing such an alliance. Henry VII accordingly arranged "suitable" marriages for each of his four children—though his efforts were not crowned with notable success.

In 1501, Arthur, the fifteen-year-old heir to the Tudor throne, had been married to Katharine of Aragon, the sixteen-year-old and youngest daughter of the Catholic Monarchs of Spain, Ferdinand and Isabella. Five months after the wedding, Arthur died. A new plan set in motion for Katharine to marry the younger son Henry (five and a half years her junior) did not materialize for seven years, not until after the death of Henry VII in 1509. As there was some doubt at the time whether church law permitted a man to marry his brother's widow, a special dispensation was sought and granted by Pope Julius II. The validity of this dispensation was not challenged until lack of a male heir, and his desire to marry Anne Boleyn, led Henry VIII to try to have his marriage to Katharine of Aragon annulled.

Margaret, Henry VII's second child, married James IV of Scotland but was left a widow when he was killed by the English at the battle of Flodden Field.

Their grandchild was Mary, Queen of Scots. By a second marriage, Margaret had a daughter, Lady Margaret Douglas, who was to become one of our Mary's closest friends.

Henry VII's younger daughter Mary had been betrothed when she was still a child to her cousin Charles (later Charles V), the son of her mother's sister Juana and Philip of the Netherlands, but this contract was broken during the reign of Henry VIII. Mary was married instead to the elderly King of France, Louis XII, who died within three months of the wedding. Mary then married the man of her own choice, Charles Brandon, Duke of Suffolk, a good friend to Henry VIII throughout his life. Their daughter Frances was the mother of Lady Jane Grey.

The marriage of Juana and Philip, arranged by Ferdinand and Isabella, brought about in theory the desired result of a dynastic marriage. Their son, Charles, governed Spain and the Spanish possessions jointly with his mother Juana (although in fact she took no share in the government as she was said to be mad and was locked away in a castle in Tordesillas). The Netherlands and Burgundy (Franche Comte) came to him from his father; and the Hapsburg Empire he inherited from his grandfather Maximilian. In practice, the territories over which he held sway were too large, too dispersed and too disparate to be governed by any one man. Charles was forced to delegate his duties to other members of his family: Spain first to his wife Isabella, then on her death to his son Philip; the Netherlands to his sister, Maria, the widowed Queen of Hungary. The Hapsburg Empire Charles handed over to his brother Ferdinand. While advising his regents on the government of his own realms, Charles was also engaged in continual military exploits against his own Protestant rebels, followers of Luther, against the Turkish invaders of Europe, against France and against the Pope. For the Pope was not just the spiritual head of the Catholic Church, he was also the political head of the Papal States, with an army to defend them. Charles was a Catholic and accepted the supremacy of the Pope in matters of religion but this did not prevent his soldiers from sacking Rome and imprisoning Pope Clement VII in 1527 nor from waging war on Pope Paul IV in 1556.

   Charles's involvement in Europe prevented him from taking any active part in the protection of his aunt Katharine of Aragon or of his cousin Mary when Henry turned against them. He gave advice and was kept informed of the situation by his ambassadors who reported to him in detail. To their dispatches and to those of the Venetian ambassadors we are indebted for many details of Mary's life we would not otherwise have known.

"Not only is she brave and valiant, unlike other timid and spiritless women, but so courageous and resolute that neither in adversity nor peril did she ever display cowardice or pusillanimity ... so that it may be said of her, as Cardinal Pole says with truth, that in the darkness and obscurity of the Kingdom she remained precisely like a feeble light, buffetted by raging winds for its utter extinction, but always kept burning, and defended by her innocence and lively faith, that it might shine in the world, as it now does shine."

MICHIEL, VENETIAN AMBASSADOR

"... After these great afflictions falling upon this realm from the beginning of Queen Mary's reign, wherein so many men, women, and children were burnt, many imprisoned and in prisons starved, divers exiled, some spoiled of goods and possessions, great number driven from house and home, so many weeping eyes, so many sobbing hearts, so many children made fatherless, so many fathers bereft of their wives and children, so many vexed in conscience, and divers against conscience constrained to recant; and, in conclusion, never a good man almost in all the realm but suffered something during this bloody persecution."

FOXE'S BOOK OF MARTYRS

*Katherine of Aragon, first Queen of Henry VIII and mother of Mary. (After Johannes Corvus.)* NATIONAL PORTRAIT GALLERY, LONDON.

# CHAPTER I

# PRINCESS MARY

## 1. First Days

On Monday, the eighteenth of February, 1516, at four o'clock in the morning, the Queen of England gave birth to a daughter. This was an event of great importance, for although her parents and the entire nation had hoped and prayed for a son and heir, a girl child was still welcome—chiefly because she was alive when born. After almost seven years of marriage, with a history of stillbirths, miscarriages and early infant deaths (including a boy who had sustained their hopes for as long as two months), King Henry VIII and his queen, Katharine of Aragon, had remained childless. As it was always possible that the new-born baby might also not have long to live, three days after her birth she was made to undergo the rite of Catholic baptism in order to prepare her for this world or the next. But, in spite of the winter cold, the considerable risk of disease at that time, her own indifferent health throughout her life and various plots which were to be hatched against her, she was to survive for forty-two years.

The baptismal ceremony took place in the richly decorated church of The Observant Friars, next to the royal palace of Greenwich, where the King and Queen were then residing. A silver font had been brought specially from Canterbury and a large wooden porch, its bare walls covered with fine tapestries, had been added to the church for the occasion. The path to be followed by the procession from palace to church was freshly gravelled and covered with rushes to protect the robes of those taking part. Preceded by the lords and gentlemen of the court, the infant princess was carried in the arms of the Countess of Surrey under a canopy supported by four knights. The two leading members of the English nobility, the Duke of Norfolk (uncle of the then little-known Anne Boleyn) and the Duke of Suffolk (Charles Brandon, the King's good friend and brother-in-law) walked one on each side. There is no mention in the records of the presence of either the King or the Queen.

The child was named Mary after, it has generally been said, the King's sister. But, Katharine may also have remembered her own sister Maria,* Queen of Portugal, whom she had not seen since they were children together in Spain. There were three godparents—the all-powerful Cardinal Wolsey, Archbishop of York; the Duchess of Norfolk; and Lady Katharine, the widowed Countess of Devonshire.**

After the baptism, the company passed into the church for Mary's confirmation. Her sponsor was Margaret Pole, Countess of Salisbury (a cousin of the King's mother), at that time a good friend of both King and Queen. According to custom, the Archbishop of Canterbury, William Warham, probably officiated at the

---

*Maria died very shortly after the birth of Mary.
**Katharine, sixth daughter of Edward IV, sister of Henry VIII's mother Elizabeth of York—"Daughter, Sister and Aunt of Kings."

services. When the last prayer had been sung, the trumpets sounded and the heralds proclaimed: "God give good life and long unto the right high, right noble and right excellent Princess Mary, Princess of England and daughter of our sovereign lord, The King."[1] The people of England were then free to celebrate the occasion with the customary processions, bonfires and feasting. As they drank the free wine which flowed in the water conduits, they may have wondered for a moment whether this time they had just cause to rejoice.

A few days later, when the Venetian ambassador congratulated the King on the birth of his daughter and also expressed his regret that she was not a boy, the King replied, "We are both young; if it be a girl this time, by the Grace of God, boys will follow."[2] It is true that Henry was still young. He was not yet twenty-four—but his wife was six years older, in poor health and weakened by continual pregnancies. The King's optimism was not to be rewarded. If it had been rewarded, the history of the rest of his reign and of the Reformation in England would have taken a different course. During the next two years the Queen had one stillborn son and one, perhaps two, stillborn daughters. Her childbearing life was then over, though this fact does not appear to have been publicly recognized until some time later.

The young Princess did not live with her parents, though she often visited them and usually spent the religious festivals such as Christmas and Easter in the palace they were occupying at the time. She was given a household and budget of her own and was moved from one royal manor to another as custom and hygiene dictated. For her first Christmas she was brought across the Thames by boat to Ditton Park, not far from Windsor Castle, where her parents were in residence. She received, as was then the practice, gifts at the New Year,

*Henry VIII, (as a young man in his early thirties.) (Artist unknown, c. 1520-25.) NATIONAL PORTRAIT GALLERY, LONDON.*

including a gold cup from her godfather, Cardinal Wolsey, and a gold pomander from her godmother, the Duchess of Suffolk. She was also given a gold spoon, two smocks and a primer, a religious book for later use.

Lady Margaret Bryan, a trusted servant of the Crown, was appointed Lady Mistress of the new household. Mary's wet nurse was Katharine Pole, a relative by marriage of the Countess of Salisbury. (It was not the habit of Tudor mothers of noble birth to nurse their own children.) In addition, Mary had her own priest, a chaplain, a clerk of the closet, and a number of servants including a laundress and four people whose task it was to rock her cradle. Among the goods which accompanied her on her move from house to house were listed such miscellaneous items as beds, sheets, woolen blankets, down pillows, carpets, a velvet chair, pewter basins, leather waterjugs and clothes brushes. Careful attention was given to Mary's diet. She and her household were served with simple food and few courses as compared with the prodigious amount of rich and varied dishes common in the royal palaces and other great houses.

When still only a few months old, Mary became a godmother, the first of many such responsibilities she was later to undertake voluntarily and conscientiously. As she was too young to attend the service, Lady Boleyn and Lady Elizabeth Grey acted as proxies for Mary and the Queen. The child they sponsored was the first daughter of the Duchess of Suffolk, Frances Brandon, who was to play an important part in Mary's later life.

There is no account of the early relationship between Mary and her mother. The Queen is not even listed as having given her daughter presents at New Year, though it is difficult to believe that this was so. It is apparent, however, from Mary's later behavior and way of life how much she was influenced by her mother's deeply religious and moral example. Katharine showed her love by careful attention to her daughter's spiritual welfare and education. This was also demonstrated by her choice of Margaret Pole, an equally devout and conscientious woman, to be Mary's godmother and, afterwards, her governess. Katharine's own upbringing did not allow her to forget that she was married to the King of England and that her first duties were toward him and her adopted country. As yet, her affections for her husband and child did not conflict.

Henry's devotion to his little daughter is more in evidence. Apart from the generous allowance he granted for the running of her household, he appears to have been a proud and doting father. Mary was said to receive more attention than the Queen when she was brought to court. The Venetian ambassador reported how Henry carried her in his arms and (in his colloquial Latin) boasted that she never cried: "Per Deum immortalem ista puella nunquam plorat."[3] Wolsey, the ambassadors and the highest officers of the court were expected to kiss her hand.

In July 1518 one of Mary's servants was taken ill and was feared to be suffering from the "sweating sickness," a deadly disease akin to a serious influenza then prevalent in England. Henry was so concerned for Mary's health that he immediately ordered her to be taken away from the risk of infection. Even when the servant was said to have recovered, Mary was still kept on the move—from Byssham Abbey to the More, to Enfield, to Havering. Although she apparently escaped the sweating sickness she was already plagued by her own brand of ill health. The following year there were rumors in France that she had died after a serious illness.

In 1520 Henry, accompanied by Katharine, went to meet the French King on the Field of Cloth of Gold.

He did not forget their daughter left behind in England. He had the lords of the Council visit her and they reported to him in France: "We were on Saturday last past at your manor of Richmond with your dearest daughter the Princess, who lauded be Almighty God, is right merry and in prosperous health and state, daily exercising herself in virtuous pastimes and occupations."[4] These pastimes included music and dancing. Encouraged by her father, who was himself a keen musician, Mary early in her life showed aptitude and promise. When at the age of two, she demanded that an Italian priest and musician who had come to show off his musical talents to the King should play for her, the priest had to comply and was then complimented by the King.* Henry indeed claimed that she played the spinet better than he did.

If anything can be deduced from these anecdotes about Mary's childhood, it is that she was a bright, gifted little girl, brought up with care and certainly with more affection than was common in families at that time. She may have appeared even more precocious than she was because she was so thin and small for her age. She was treated with great ceremony when she came to court and her own household revolved around her. In her earliest days she must have taken for granted her own importance in her own small world. She was an English royal princess with no brothers or sisters to share the considerable attention and many privileges bestowed upon her.

---

*The detailed account of this episode was considered important enough to be reported back home by the Venetians.

*The Emperor Charles V, cousin of Mary. (Studio of Van Orley.)*

## 2. Early Marriage Plans

From the moment of her birth, Mary became negotiable. As the daughter of a royal house, Mary was expected to make a dynastic marriage, as her parents had done, which would consolidate a treaty of friendship between England and another European country. Charles V, Francis I, the Dauphin, the Duke of Orleans, the Duke of Milan were only some of the bridegrooms suggested for Mary in her childhood. The most important allies to be cultivated were France or Spain, depending on their relative strength at any moment, for it was important to Henry to maintain the balance of power in Europe. But this happened to be a bad time for finding a bridegroom in either of these countries. Francis, the King of France, was two years younger than Henry and he had as yet no children. Spain had been in a turmoil since the death of Ferdinand in 1516. The heir to the Spanish throne was Katharine's sister Juana, widowed Queen of Philip of the Netherlands. But Juana was moody after the death of her husband, some said mad, and she was considered unfit to rule. Her eldest son Charles was only sixteen and it remained to be seen whether he could control and reunite a country split by its warring nobles.

Charles had already been betrothed to Henry's sister Mary, in 1507, when he was seven and she eleven years old, but this engagement had been broken off by the English in favor of a French alliance. While it was possible that after such treatment Charles himself did not wish for another English betrothal, it had never been unusual to play off one country against another. Present contingencies counted for more than old affronts. Six months after Mary was born there was a report in England that a match between Mary and her cousin Charles had been suggested but no action seems to have been taken.

In 1517 the French Queen became pregnant, and the news soon spread across the Channel. The possibility of a betrothal between Mary and the unborn child, should it turn out to be a son, was at once discussed by the pro-French faction in England. The child was born in 1518, and it was a boy. Negotiations were immediately set in train which culminated six months later in the signing of a treaty between the two countries, followed by great feasting and rejoicing. The next day, in an elaborate betrothal ceremony in Greenwich Palace, Mary became Princess of France as well as of England. One of the most graphic descriptions of Mary as a young child is on this occasion of her first betrothal when she was two and a half years old. Dressed like a miniature adult, she wore a long robe of cloth of gold and, on her fair curls, a black velvet cap glistening with jewels. She was carried in by a nurse and then stood with her father and pregnant mother while she was solemnly betrothed to the infant Dauphin of France, for whom the Earl of Surrey stood proxy. The Venetian account of the occasion relates that Mary then wanted to kiss the Admiral of France, thinking this was the man she was to marry.

In spite of her ingrained pro-Spanish sympathies, Queen Katharine gave her public assent to the betrothal. Afterwards, however, she tried to arrange a meeting between Henry and her nephew Charles with the intention of breaking the French alliance. Her point of view gained support when, a month after the ceremony at Greenwich, she lost the hoped-for son she had been carrying. The pleasant thought that the English Princess should become Queen of France was now superseded by the fear that the Dauphin might become King of England.

Katharine's desire was for a treaty of friendship with Spain, cemented by the betrothal of Charles and Mary. This was more important to her than the sixteen-year disparity of age between the cousins. It was a natural sequence to her own dynastic marriage. Charles came to England twice, once briefly in 1520 and then on a state visit in 1522 when he met Mary, by all accounts a charming child of six, for the first, and only, time.* It looked as though Katharine's wish was to be fulfilled. Mary was officially betrothed to Charles, again at Greenwich, and the marriage treaty contained the clause that if they should have a son he would inherit the throne of England. Once more there was an excuse for celebration and expensive pageantry.

The French betrothal was allowed to lapse, though it was never officially annulled. This caused no great surprise to Francis, who was well aware of the discussions that had been taking place with Charles during the previous four years. And the betrothal to Charles did not prevent Henry from receiving envoys from Scotland trying to negotiate a union between James V (son of Henry's other sister Margaret) and Mary. This plan did not mature either for, though Margaret would have liked the match between the cousins, the Scottish people were lukewarm.

Katharine had been instrumental in bringing Henry and Charles together, but the new betrothal cound not be attributed to her influence alone. Circumstances had changed since 1516. It was now accepted that the English Queen would bear no more children and Henry had recognized Mary as his heir. The fear of a French king on the English throne was thereby strengthened. Charles, on the other hand, had become

*Blossom Inn, in the City of London, stands on the site of the old inn where accommodation was provided for ten of Charles's followers and stabling for twenty of his horses.

much more acceptable. He was no longer an untried boy. Although not popular in Spain, he had consolidated his position vis-à-vis the nobles and had taken over complete control from his mother Juana who remained joint ruler only in name. The considerable riches of the newly discovered lands in the west were his. (To emphasize this point, he had brought with him to the English Court some of Montezuma's treasure.) He governed Burgundy and the Netherlands as well as the Hapsburg territories. And a combination of heredity and bribery had ensured his election as Emperor in his grandfather Maximilian's place in 1519, in spite of considerable opposition from Francis and Henry. It was not yet evident that the extensive bribery in which he had indulged had brought him into a state of indebtedness from which he was never to extricate himself.

However, in spite of all the advantages possessed by Charles, this marriage plan fared no better than its French predecessor. Henry quarreled with Charles. When Charles asked that Mary be sent to the court of Margaret of Savoy (where he himself had been brought up) to be educated in Spanish ways, Henry refused, saying that Mary was his own treasure and that of his kingdom. The romantic notion that Henry really did not want to send his only beloved child out of the country may have had some truth in it. In any case, Charles had become too powerful. Henry again flirted with Francis.

Charles himself had much less to gain from the marriage. Not only was his intended bride still a young child, but he had already borrowed and spent on his army the equivalent of the dowry he had agreed with Henry. He could look forward to no further supplies of money from that source. He was also being pressed to marry another cousin, Isabella, the daughter of Maria of Portugal, who was nearer his own age and brought with her a larger dowry. After much formal bickering between the two rulers, Charles broke off his betrothal to Mary and early in 1526 married Isabella.

At the age of nine, Mary had already been officially betrothed twice. Thereafter, her marriage prospects fluctuated considerably as Henry continued to use her as diplomatic bait, which he did until the end of his life. Nothing came of any of his betrothal schemes and perhaps he never intended that anything should. The English people were said to be against any foreign bridegroom, fearing that he might usurp the functions of king, and also against any English bridegroom because he would not be of royal blood. Mary had as yet expressed no opinion that has been recorded and indeed, at this time, had no choice in the matter. She wrote to Charles and an emerald was sent in her name as a present to him. But the betrothal business for her as a child was purely academic. It is unlikely, though possible, that she felt elated when betrothed or distressed when a betrothal lapsed.

The increasing power of the Emperor in Europe encouraged Henry to try to turn the scales against him. Two years after the break with Charles, Henry appeared to be considering marrying his much-loved young daughter to the newly-widowed and reputed rake Francis, nineteen years her senior. The French ambassador came to the English court to inspect her and negotiate the treaty. Mary was made to show off her considerable talents in French and Latin, music and dancing. Her tiny figure was decked out in fine robes and she was decorated with costly jewels. At one of the lavish entertainments provided for the French envoys, Henry affectionately pulled off Mary's cap so that "a profusion of silver tresses, as beautiful as ever seen on human head, fell over her shoulders, forming a most agreeable sight."[5] But the Venetian who reported the scene said that Mary was so thin and small that the French did not think she could be married for another three years.

The betrothal did not take place, however, because of the pressure brought to bear on Francis by the Emperor. Charles who had taken Francis prisoner at the battle of Pavia in 1525 demanded that his own sister, Eleanor, should become Queen of France. The French King had to submit but, as he was not averse to having the English as allies against his enemy he then suggested his second son, Henry, Duke of Orleans, as a suitable candidate for Mary's hand.

Henry's sincerity in such negotiations may be doubtful, but he was seriously concerned about the English succession. England had long been governed by kings—whether to the good or not was not to the point. To have a queen on the throne was in itself an unwelcome thought; it was even worse to think that whoever married Mary would have too powerful a position in the country, whether the title he held was that of king or consort. So Henry also looked around nearer home. Although, with hindsight, an alliance with Scotland by a marriage to James V would seem to have been the best solution, Henry did not pursue it. A more far-fetched idea occurred to him. He thought, or had it suggested to him, that in order to resolve his dilemma he should himself marry again, this time to a young woman who would be expected to provide him with a son. Mary's marriage would then be of secondary importance in regard to the succession. But in order to marry again Henry had to find a good reason for getting rid of the wife he already had. It was at this point that he began to question the legality of his marriage to his brother's widow.*

*See *Introduction*, p. 1.

Already in 1525, the Archbishop of Canterbury, William Warham, knew what was on Henry's mind, but it was not until May 17, 1527, that Henry started proceedings to have his marriage annulled. The Archbishop of Canterbury and Thomas Wolsey, Archbishop of York, charged him at a secret court with having lived in sin with his brother's widow. Afraid of public reaction Henry tried to conceal his plan, but news of "The King's Great Matter" quickly leaked to Katharine, to the English people and to the continent. How much Mary knew of what was happening can only be guessed.

Katharine put up a strong opposition and had powerful supporters. She refused to accept Henry's request that she should retire quietly to a convent. She was not amenable to any demand which would entail separation from Henry with a resultant change in her own status as Queen and in Mary's as Princess and heir to the throne. She would not admit that she had been living in sin for eighteen years and the corollary that Mary was illegitimate. Henry, by some curious logic, could believe his daughter to be legitimate even while insisting that he had never been legally married to her mother. The Duke of Norfolk, certainly echoing the sentiments of the people and presumably of the King, perhaps even of his own though he was Anne Boleyn's uncle, was later reported as saying "The Princess would never be married except in a high position, for she was still heiress of the kingdom; and when the great affair was settled in the King's favour, and he remarried, it was uncertain whether he would have male children, and, if not, she would be preferred to other daughters. If any person ventured to say that she was illegitimate, he would have his head cut off."[6]

At first Henry did not seem to have had any particular replacement for Katharine in mind. But Anne Boleyn arrived on the scene at the crucial moment.

What might have been another ephemeral affair had become, by the fall of 1527, a serious business with a view to marriage. The details of the protracted proceedings which enabled Henry to marry Anne Boleyn in 1533 and have his marriage to Katharine annulled concern us here only as far as they affected Mary. They covered the period from when she was eleven years old to when she was seventeen, six important formative years of her life.

During the course of the so-called "divorce"* negotiations, another bridegroom was suggested for Mary, a choice particularly distressing to her mother. A few years after Mary was born Henry had recognized as his illegitimate son a child born to Elizabeth Blount, one of the Queen's young maids of honor. In 1527 he considered the possibility of getting a dispensation from the Pope to allow this boy, Henry Fitzroy, to marry his half-sister, thus ensuring the throne for both Henry's children. The Pope was reported as not being averse to the idea, but was not in fact approached officially. Henry may have been justifiably afraid of the reaction of the English people to such an arrangement.

## 3. Education

The various marriage plans for Mary had not been allowed to interfere with her lessons. As a little girl she had shown that she had already been well instructed in Latin as well as the more joyous accomplishments of music and dancing. A more masculine approach was made to her upbringing than was usual for girls of her time, though the feminine and religious aspects were by no means neglected. One of the results of

*It was not *divorce* Henry sought but *annulment* of the marriage on the grounds that Katharine had previously been married to his brother.

the Renaissance was the foundation of many schools for boys with a broad curriculum including Latin and Greek. But some of the Humanist scholars—Linacre, More, Vives, Erasmus—believed that girls should also be educated. Mary benefited from the new ideas and was taught much more than the domestic accomplishments usually considered sufficient for a girl in the early sixteenth century. In this respect, she was also fortunate in having educated parents who not only encouraged learning at home but also invited foreign scholars to visit England. Erasmus expressed his admiration when he said that the royal court was more like a home for the Muses. Henry and Katharine gave much thought both to the way in which their daughter should be taught and what kind of subjects she should study. The ideas of Sir Thomas More in particular were a great influence on them and the way he brought up his children was an example to be followed.

Mary's first tutor was said to be Linacre, a scholar as well as an eminent doctor. He had been physician to Henry VII and to Wolsey and had been Prince Arthur's tutor in 1501. He was now nearing the end of his life. He died in 1524. It is unlikely that he actually taught Mary himself, but he revised his Latin grammar (written in English) and dedicated a copy to Mary.* Katharine herself helped Mary with her Latin until she was nine years old and must have encouraged her to pursue her studies in other subjects too. We know Mary learned French and Italian and, from her mother and her mother's Spanish ladies, she learned some Spanish. In later years she said she could understand the language though she could not speak it.

But in 1525 a great change came in Mary's life. The King decided to honor his legitimate and illegiti-

---

*This book can still be seen in the British Museum.

mate offspring at the same time. Titles were heaped on
the seven-year-old Henry Fitzroy. He was made Duke
of Richmond (a title which had formerly belonged to
Henry VII) and first peer of the realm, second only to
the King—which could have indicated that Henry had
him in mind for the succession. He was then sent with a
company of important nobles to govern the northern
part of the country bordering on Scotland. Mary was
sent with a retinue of over three hundred people to the
Welsh border. She was called Princess of Wales, and she
lived at Ludlow Castle and at Tickenhill, which was repaired and put in order for her arrival. A special Council
was appointed to carry out the duties of governing the
area. Mary's private establishment was increased and its
control entrusted to the Countess of Salisbury.* Katharine, Countess of Devonshire, was chief of Mary's
ladies-in-waiting.

Dr. Richard Fetherstone became Mary's resident
tutor, an appointment recommended by the Spanish
scholar Vives in whom Katharine had great faith. Vives
himself may not have disapproved of Mary's removal
from Henry's noisy and licentious court environment,
fearing it might not be altogether balanced by her
mother's quiet and religious circle. He believed that
girls should be protected from temptation. If the anec-
dote told by the author of *Jane Dormer*[7] is accurate,
Henry himself could not believe that his daughter was
so different from the ladies at his own court. He sent Sir
Francis Brian to test whether she really "knew no foul
or unclean speeches" and was assured that it was true.
Katharine's influence was stronger in regard to religious
and moral values, but Henry's pleasure in fine clothes,

*The Countess of Salisbury, as Margaret Pole, had also accompanied Kath-
arine of Aragon to Wales in 1501, when she and Prince Arthur had been
sent by Henry VII to govern the border country.

in music and dancing, and his enjoyment of gambling were all reflected in his daughter.

The Countess of Salisbury and the Council were carefully instructed in matters relating to Mary's education, health, dress, food and amusements. Mary was to learn Latin, French, Italian and Greek, rhetoric and philosophy. She was to read the Bible, but only selected portions. Among contemporary authors she was permitted Erasmus and Sir Thomas More. She was encouraged to take moderate outdoor exercise in fair and healthy places. Riding was not mentioned specifically, but she had been accustomed to horses all her life, first as a baby to be carried in a litter between two horses, then, as soon as she was able to ride, side-saddle. Hunting was a common sport even for children. It was stipulated that her dress should be simple but clean, her food plain but well-prepared and eaten in "joyous ... and virtuous manner." Everything about her was to be "pure, sweet, clean and wholesome, and as to so great a princess does appertain, and all corruptions, evil airs, and things noisome and displeasant to be foreborn and eschewed."[8]

Although Vives frowned on frivolous pursuits, Henry may have believed that his daughter should be happy and healthy as well as pious and learned. She was encouraged to do her needlework, to dance and to play the virginals (a small keyboard instrument like a spinet but especially suitable for girls) and lute, occupations at which she excelled and in which she apparently took great pleasure. At the Christmas festivities, most elaborate mummeries and entertainments were devised for her pleasure and that of her ladies, although she was not yet quite ten years old.

As the company of a few other girls of similar age to share her lessons was recommended, it is likely that some accompanied Mary to the Welsh border. One of them is known to have been Lady Katharine Grey. Another may have been her cousin Lady Margaret Douglas, who long continued to be one of Mary's friends.

How much Mary was aware of the growing rift between her parents and of the existence and honoring of Henry Fitzroy is not known. As she had her own household and did not spend a great deal of time at court, some of the current gossip could have been kept from her childish ears. It is possible that she had seen Henry Fitzroy, perhaps on the occasion when he received his honors. But she must have been aware of her mother's serious illnesses and have known when Katharine was temporarily banished from court. This is evident from a letter written by Katharine to Mary in Ludlow when she says that "the long absence of the King and you troubleth me" and that her health is only "metely good."⁹

Mary's sojourn in Wales did not last long, though the Council remained. Henry made a special effort to see her at Langley in 1526, when there was a serious epidemic of the sweating sickness, and she visited her parents at Ampthill shortly afterwards. It seems as though Wolsey acted as intermediary between father and daughter. In a letter of thanks written to him by Mary, in Latin, she says: "I confess myself much indebted to your right reverend sanctity, both for your welcome letters delivered to me at the palace of Ampthill and more especially that it is by your late intercession that I have been allowed for a month to enjoy, to my supreme delight, the society of the king and queen my parents: the health of both of whom may the great Sovereign of kings crown with enduring felicity."¹⁰

Mary's book of accounts for the period when she was in residence in Wales ended at the close of the same year. Her reappearance at court and presence in England were necessitated by her father's plans to marry her to Francis.* During the accompanying festivities, after hearing her speak in French, Latin and English and perform on the virginals, one of Francis's ambassadors said that she was the most accomplished child he had ever seen. Richard Sampson, the Dean of Windsor, described her about this time as having a sweet seriousness and being joyous and decorous. Up to the age of eleven, her life had indeed been joyous. Even if disciplined, she was treated with love and affection by her parents and governess and highly esteemed by all who met her. But, with the advent of Anne Boleyn, this was all to change.

## 4. Separation

At first, Anne Boleyn's rise to favor did not bring about a great change in the Queen's way of life. Katharine had long since absented herself from the daily round of gaiety at court but, when a public appearance at festivities was necessary, as at Christmas, she was present and welcomed. She accepted the fact that Henry amused himself without her. She was glad to see him when he visited her. She sewed his shirts on occasion and gave him advice, as she had always been accustomed to do. Sometimes, when her obstinacy in regard to the "divorce" infuriated Henry more than usual, she was banished from his presence and was not allowed to communicate with him in any way, but she was not prevented from returning when his anger diminished. Little by little, however, her influence was eroded. By 1529, all that remained of their marriage was the public façade.

After 1527, there are fewer references to her in the records. For Mary the change was more immediately

*See page 13.

obvious. Her appearances at court became fewer and eventually ceased altogether. She saw less of both her parents and must have asked why. What answers she received or what gossip was fed to her we do not know. We only know that she felt ill. Always, when she was particularly unhappy, it was reflected in her physical condition: her digestion was upset and she suffered from hysteria. The two people she loved most and depended on most were no longer available to give her the support she so badly needed. Katharine loved her daughter but she firmly believed that, if the choice had to be made, her duty was to stay by her husband's side. Even though Anne was in residence with him too, Katharine did not believe that she was there permanently. But she could take no risks. Mary's future could only be safeguarded if Katharine herself retained her position as Queen. Katharine had no idea that the outcome of this affair of Henry's was to be different from any of the others. Sometimes she was extremely pessimistic, at others cheerful and optimistic. She had greater faith in her nephew and the Pope than was warranted by their ability to be of assistance. She trusted that with God's help, and theirs, life would soon return to normal: that Henry would treat her as before, that his paramour would go the way of her predecessors, and that Mary would be free to come to court again, the undoubted legitimate heir to the throne.

During these troubled times Mary's education was not altogether neglected. With the King's permission, Vives had gone home to see his family in 1527, but had been invited to return in the fall. The Queen, fearful for the future, pressed him to come back "to teach the most illustrious lady princess the Latin language and such precepts of wisdom as would arm her against any adverse fortune."[11] Life was made so difficult for him, however, because of Henry's suspicions of his friendship with Katharine, that he did not stay long on his second visit. On his departure, Dr. Fetherstone seems still to have been in charge of Mary's studies. The Countess of Salisbury continued to supervise her general upbringing and to encourage the same moral qualities which Katharine would have wished. She was as devoted to her charge as she would have been if Mary had been her own granddaughter.

Anne Boleyn disliked the Queen and was impatient and angry that Katharine's tactics deferred her own promotion but she reluctantly allowed Henry to visit his wife because she knew that no affection, only habit, was involved. As much as Katharine hoped and trusted in a restoration of the status quo, Anne Boleyn believed that the time would come eventually when she would be Queen of England. Of Mary, however, Anne Boleyn was genuinely jealous and afraid. She knew that Henry was still devoted to his daughter. The real affection he had felt for the little girl survived into her teens. He did not, as yet, include his daughter in the anger he felt toward his wife for refusing to cooperate. Anne Boleyn did everything in her power to poison their relationship and to prevent any meeting between father and daughter. On the whole she was successful, but sometimes she failed—and these occasions were sufficiently remarkable to be noted by the Emperor's ambassador. Once when Mary was ill and he was hunting in her neighborhood, Henry called in twice a day for a week. But later on, when she was ill again and asked to be allowed to see her father and mother, Henry refused her plea.

In July 1531, matters came to a climax. Henry and Anne Boleyn went out hunting together, leaving Katharine behind at Windsor, a not unusual occurrence in itself. But this time they did not return. Henry and Katharine never saw each other again. Unaware that this was the case and thinking to take advantage of Anne

Boleyn's absence, Katharine sent for Mary to come and visit her. Mother and daughter also went hunting and visiting the neighborhood. For a short while it would seem that they were relaxed and that the time passed as pleasantly as it could. Katharine wrote to Henry but he did not reply. Then came Henry's command that Katharine was to leave Windsor before his return. She had no choice but to obey. Katharine was sent to the More, a royal house, and Mary was sent to the palace of Richmond. Here she was visited by some Venetians who reported: "This Princess is not tall, has a pretty face, and is well proportioned, with a very beautiful complexion, and is fifteen years old. She speaks Spanish, French and Latin, besides her own mother-English tongue, is well grounded in Greek, and understands Italian, but does not venture to speak it. She sings excellently, and plays on several instruments, so that she combines every accomplishment."[12] Another Venetian writing back home emphasized what had been said by others, that the King was not popular in the country because of his behavior toward his wife, who was much loved. The Queen retained the affection and sympathy of the English people until the end of her life. Mary too was held in high regard at this time and was much loved and respected.

It is doubtful whether Katharine and Mary ever met again. Mary's reaction was as usual expressed in terms of health: she was ill for the rest of that year. At first, mother and daughter were able to write to each other openly, then secretly when that became necessary. In 1532, Henry thought he had put an end to their correspondence. When he discovered that they still managed to exchange letters, he took steps to make it impossible. If it had not been for the presence of Eustace Chapuys, Charles's ambassador who had arrived in England in August 1529, they would not have been able to communicate in any way. As long as he was allowed to see them he could carry verbal messages, but the time was to come when Chapuys was forbidden to visit either of them. He still saw much of the contemporary scene, however, even if from a biased point of view. It is from his lengthy dispatches to the Emperor that we learn much of the sad history of Katharine and Mary at this time.

Henry continued to give minor presents to Mary until 1532. In the September following his parting from Katharine he gave instructions to the Master of the Wardrobe that his sixteen-year-old daughter should be equipped with several splendid dresses—of silver tissue, purple velvet, black tinsel, crimson satin lined with cloth of gold, black velvet lined with ermine—and all the accessories, including sixteen pairs of velvet shoes. Even so, Henry's accounts show that he gave to his daughter in one year scarcely one-fifth of what he gave Anne Boleyn in one day.[13]

During the same month Henry met his daughter by accident: "Eight days ago the King met the Princess in the fields, but did not say much to her, except to ask how she was, and assure her that in future he would see her more often. It is certain that the King dares not bring her where the Lady is, for she does not wish to see her or hear of her."[14] He might, says Chapuys, have talked longer and more familiarly if Anne had not sent two of her people to listen to what was being said. It was evident that his infatuation with Anne, or his fear of her bad temper, was greater than his affection for Mary.

Katharine received no more presents from her husband. On the contrary, he demanded that she should give up her jewels for him to bestow upon Anne. She demurred with rather forcible language, but had to comply. The King's sister Mary also had to part with her jewels for the same purpose. When Katharine had to accept the fact that Henry had left her for good, she still refused all attempts to make her admit that her marriage was not legal. The proceedings begun by Henry and hindered by her dragged on for another eighteen months. Wolsey, the all-powerful arch-enemy whom Katharine had blamed (rightly or wrongly) for starting Henry on this course, had fallen from grace because he had not been able to bring it to a successful conclusion. His high state offices had been taken from him and his considerable wealth confiscated. He died at the end of 1530 before any of the trumped-up charges devised by his enemies, with Anne's encouragement and Henry's acquiescence, could be brought against him in a court of law. Sir Thomas More became Chancellor in his place, but only held the position for two years before resigning it of his own free will. Thomas Cromwell, one of Wolsey's own loyal men, was to succeed his master as Katharine's chief adversary. His Machiavellian genius proved more successful in finding a means to end the divorce proceedings. He was then able to consolidate his position until, as First Secretary, he too became the real power behind the throne.

Against Henry's wishes and command, Katharine appealed directly to the Pope to declare that her marriage was legal. Wifely disobedience could be justified when her husband was trying to declare that she was not his wife. By having the case decided in Rome, she hoped to get the justice she believed to be denied her in England. Above all, she wished to prevent Henry from declaring Mary illegitimate. But by this very appeal she pushed Henry into a course of action which was to have more far-reaching results than either of them could have anticipated. Henry was driven to deny the authority of the Pope, the recognized Head of the Church in all Christendom. After putting intense pressure upon the English clergy, with Cromwell's connivance, Henry had

*Thomas Cromwell, Earl of Essex, Secretary to Henry VIII. Beheaded
1540. (Hans Holbein.)* THE FRICK COLLECTION, NEW YORK.

them declare the King to be Head of the Church in England.

When people were slow to express approval of his new measure, Henry exacted obedience by force. If this failed, the ultimate penalty was imposed. Fear was so strong that even the great had few supporters. Fisher, the Bishop of Rochester, was sent to the Tower and then beheaded. Sir Thomas More refused to commit himself in words. This legal quibble did not save him and he suffered the same fate. Cromwell tried to persuade him to submit to the King's will, as did his wife, but in vain. His last reputed words, "I die the King's good servant, but God's first,"[15] have passed into history. The apparent ease with which these martyrs gave up their lives indicated their profound belief in the world to come.

Warham, who had supported Henry against Katharine, died in 1532, acknowledging on his deathbed that he had erred. The following year he was succeeded as Archbishop of Canterbury by Thomas Cranmer, another supporter of the King who could be relied upon to work in harness with Cromwell. Their first task was to make good Wolsey's failure: to achieve the annulment of Henry's marriage to Katharine. And there was now need for haste. Anne Boleyn had taken over Katharine's place in everything but name. But her position was ambiguous as long as she was not married, and Katharine refused to give up the title of Queen. Early in 1533, Anne announced that she was pregnant. When she had at last consented to become Henry's mistress is not known. She and Henry were married in order to make the expected son and heir legitimate, but the marriage was kept secret.

By the Act of Appeals, passed in March, all legal power, both spiritual and temporal, was vested in the hands of the King, thus making it impossible for anyone to appeal to any court outside the country. This meant that the Pope's decision on the legality of Henry's marriage would now have no validity in England and Katharine had no further redress. In May, Cranmer summoned Katharine to a court held in Dunstable, near Ampthill where she was then living. She refused to attend and was declared contumacious. In her absence, on May 23, Cranmer declared her marriage to Henry invalid. A few days later he declared that the marriage

*Thomas Cranmer, Protestant Archbishop of Canterbury during reign of Henry VIII. Imprisoned on Mary's accession. Burned at the stake 1556. (Attributed Gerlach Flicke 1546.)* NATIONAL PORTRAIT GALLERY, LONDON.

*Ann Boleyn, second Queen of Henry VIII, mother of Elizabeth. Beheaded May, 1536. (Artist unknown.)* NATIONAL PORTRAIT GALLERY, LONDON.

between Henry and Anne was legal, though he did not say when it had taken place. On June 1, Anne was crowned Queen of England, with no great enthusiasm on the part of the people. The King and his new Queen then had only three months to wait for the birth of the son promised by the chief soothsayers of the realm. On September 7, the child was born. Disappointingly for both parents, and for the nation, it was another girl. She survived and was given the name Elizabeth. There was no public celebration of the event.

From the moment of Anne's victory Katharine's already deteriorating way of life became worse. She now had to accept that Henry had left her for good, that he would never take her back as Queen. She absolutely refused to accept the title of Princess Dowager, assigned to her as the widow of Prince Arthur, when attempts were made to force it upon her. In her moment of power, Anne was not to be restrained in her vindictiveness against the Spaniards whom she had once wished at the bottom of the sea. There were rumors that the lives of both Katharine and her daughter were in danger.

Katharine had appealed often and insistently to her nephew to come to her assistance and she continued to bombard him with pleas. He was sympathetic toward his aunt and cousin in their distress, of which he was kept informed by Chapuys, but there was little he could do to support them unless he declared war on England. This he was reluctant to do at a time when he had, as always, other troubles to contend with in his Empire. So Katharine had only her prayers and her tears as solace. Such friends as were left were unable and too afraid to be of assistance. Katharine's household and income were cut and she was kept under close surveillance, the equivalent of house arrest. Her health suffered and her indomitable courage almost failed.

Mary had a few months' grace before Anne had her way with her. Her income was not at first cut. In October 1533 her establishment still consisted of 162 people, including the Countess of Salisbury, Dr. Fetherstone, Lady Margaret Douglas and Lord Hussey and his wife. Her religious needs were attended to by two chaplains. She resided in New Hall (sometimes known as Beaulieu) in Essex, a mansion of some size and importance. But she was fully aware of the seriousness of her situation and distressed by her mother's absence and what she heard of the conditions of her mother's life. Her health suffered, as it always did when she was under stress and unhappy. The same rumors that reached Katharine no doubt reached her too. Both mother and daughter could only wait to see what form Anne's revenge and hatred would take now that she was in power.

# CHAPTER II

# THE LADY MARY

## 1. Out of Favor

After Elizabeth had been christened, a herald proclaimed her Princess of England. Lord Hussey, Mary's chamberlain, had the unpleasant task of asking his mistress to give up her title and bestow it upon her half-sister. Mary refused with all the dignity and obstinacy she had acquired from her mother. She wrote to her father, objecting to the title of Lady Mary, which she had been told was now hers. She would not believe he was responsible for the change. She ended her letter to him by saying that if she accepted the implication that she had not been born in true matrimony she would be offending God. Her dilemma lay between her duty to her God and to her father.

Henry was angered by Mary's attitude as much as he had been by her mother's refusal to accept the title of Princess Dowager when attempts were made to force it upon her. He therefore tried other measures to break Mary's spirit. In December, the Earls of Oxford, Essex and Sussex came to New Hall with a document entitled

**ENGLAND**

**16th CENTURY**

*Articles to be proponed and shown on our behalf to our daughter, the Lady Mary* which they said she was to read. In this paper, Henry expressed his surprise that she could continue "arrogantly to usurp the title of Princess, pretending to be heir apparent."[1] In order to prevent her pernicious example from spreading, the bearers of the document were to declare to her the folly of her conduct. She had deserved the King's high displeasure and punishment by law, but if she conformed to his will, he might incline his fatherly pity to promote her welfare.

A well-known dramatic letter of advice and encouragement from Katharine most probably dates from this same period. Rumors of some plot concerning Mary had reached her ears, though whether they referred to a possible attempt on Mary's life or to her imminent removal from New Hall is not clear. In the letter, Mary was told to obey her father in all things, "save only that you will not offend God or lose your own soul"[2]—a precept Mary was already having trouble in fulfilling. She was then asked to keep her mind and body chaste and not to desire any husband until these troublesome times were over.

Chapuys had also heard that Mary was to leave New Hall. He was asked by Katharine and Mary to speak to Cromwell on their behalf, but he knew it would be in vain. To prepare Mary to cope with the situation when it arose, he wrote down several candid and temperate statements for her to learn by heart so that she could address them to the people who came to carry out her father's orders. He and Katharine were determined that she should not do anything to prejudice her rights. She should obey her father but make it clear in so doing that she was acting under compulsion. Chapuys also prepared a secret document of formal protest which she was to sign in case of need.

As a result of Mary's recalcitrance and Chapuys's interference, which had begun to irritate him, Henry indeed withdrew all signs of fatherly pity. He had until then occasionally indicated that his love for his daughter was not entirely dead, in spite of Anne's efforts to influence him. But now he showed his anger in a concrete way. First, her household was reduced, then disbanded altogether on the pretext that its members had encouraged her in her disobedience. The threat to remove her from New Hall was put into effect—and the house was immediately taken over by Lord Rochford, Anne's brother. The Duke of Norfolk, Anne's uncle, came with others to inform her that she was to go into service with the "Princess," whose first private establishment had just been set up at Hatfield, about seventeen miles away. When Mary tried to argue that she was the only Princess, the Duke said he had not come there to dispute with her but to accomplish the King's will. Realizing she was beaten, Mary withdrew to her chamber to sign the document Chapuys had prepared for her if she was compelled to renounce her rights. Her state of mind can only be imagined.

Mary then returned, ready to obey the Duke's demands as there was no alternative that would obtain for her any better treatment. She only asked, with her customary thoughtfulness for others, that her servants should be given at least one year's wages on their dismissal. The Countess of Salisbury begged to be allowed to accompany her with a suitable train at her own expense but, not surprisingly, her request was refused. Mary was to be removed from all the old influences. She was put in a litter and carried away to Hatfield, accompanied by a very small suite. Chapuys said only two servants went with her. By her side rode Dr. Fox, the King's Almoner, who had been sent to guide her and to prevent any excessive show of indignation by the people along the way. Although he should have supported his master, he congratulated Mary on the attitude she had taken and implored her to remain firm. According to Anne Boleyn, as Mary passed through the villages she was greeted as if she were God Himself who had descended from heaven. Queen Katharine and Mary had always been very much loved and esteemed by the English people, who did not hesitate to show loyalty and affection to them even when they were out of favor. For this reason, their public appearances were first restricted and then prohibited altogether.

On Mary's arrival at Hatfield, she was asked to go and pay her respects to the "Princess." Still struggling to maintain her own status, she said that she knew no other Princess but herself. But, she continued, as her father had recognized the daughter of Anne Boleyn as his child, she was willing to call her "sister" as she called the Duke of Richmond (Henry Fitzroy) "brother." When asked what message she would send to her father, she said, "Nothing else except that his daughter, the Princess, begged his blessing."[3] (The message was not transmitted.) Remembering too the instructions she had learned, she repeated several times that what she did under duress should not prejudice her rights. Then, exhausted by the strain, she retired to her room to weep which, according to Chapuys, she did continually.

One day Henry came to visit Elizabeth. Pressed by Anne, he sent instructions that Mary was to be kept away from him. Perhaps he too was afraid, as Anne was, that his heart would melt when he saw Mary; or perhaps he realized that if she remained stubborn his anger could not easily be restrained. Instead, Cromwell was sent to remonstrate with her. But all his arguments could not win her over. "They were deceived if they thought that rudeness, bad treatment, or even the chance of death would shake her determination"[4] —

again echoes of her mother! Mary asked if she could come to kiss her father's hand, but he refused her request. As he was leaving and about to mount his horse, he happened to look up and saw a solitary, pathetic figure kneeling in a position of prayer on the terrace at the top of the house. He bowed toward her and put his hand to his hat. That was the only recognition she received. But the French ambassador, according to Chapuys, said that Henry had tears in his eyes and could not refrain from praising his daughter when recounting the story of his visit.

Shortly afterward, Anne also visited her daughter. She summoned Mary to come and pay her respects to the Queen, promising to intercede with the King on her behalf if she was obedient. But Mary maintained her intransigent attitude saying she knew no Queen in England but her mother. Anne was furious. She went away swearing to break the haughtiness of this unbridled Spanish blood. Henry was not encouraged to mitigate the treatment of his elder daughter.

In 1534 Parliament passed the *Act of Succession*, by which the children of the King and his new Queen were made heirs to the throne and Mary was uncompromisingly and legally declared a bastard. About the same time, the Pope in Rome at last declared the marriage of Henry VIII and Katharine of Aragon to be valid.* Though Katharine and Mary were now justified in believing that their souls were saved from eternal damnation, it made no difference to their lives on earth.

Since Warham's announcement to the clergy in Convocation in 1531 that the King was "their only and supreme lord and, as far as the law of Christ allows also supreme head,"[5] Parliament had been used by Cromwell to undermine by legal means the power of the Pope in England. Henry's original aim in agreeing to such

*See page 135.

measures was to secure the annulment of his marriage to Katharine without having recourse to Rome. He had no intention of denying his religion. But Cromwell had a philosophical concern with the future status of England which went deeper than the settlement of the King's marital problem. Cromwell was definitely a Protestant, but it is not clear how far his actions were determined by religious belief or how far they were politically inspired. He upheld the supremacy of the King and used Parliament to end the power of the Pope in England. He was then prepared to go even further and to acknowledge the King as supreme Head of State independent of Parliament. He himself was more than willing to act as the King's agent in both secular and lay capacities.

Various measures were passed to curtail the fiscal and legal authority of the Church and to prevent papal interference, culminating in 1534 in the *Act of Supremacy,* which made Henry *Supreme Head of the Church in England.* This was followed by the *Statute of Treasons,* which made denial of the King's supremacy punishable by death. Katharine's supporters either lost their lives, like Fisher and More, or were too afraid of the penalty to speak up on her behalf or Mary's. But their hatred of the King's measures was no less real because suppressed. Some of Mary's old friends were harassed and imprisoned in the Tower for no other reason than visiting her and continuing to use her old title. Among them was Lady Hussey, who excused herself by saying that the words slipped from her mouth from habit, not deliberately.

There were the customary movements of Elizabeth's establishment from house to house. At first Mary refused to travel with Elizabeth, as she would have to take an inferior place. This objection was answered by placing Mary in her litter and taking her by force. She then took advantage of being allowed outside the house to make a public protest en route. This gained her nothing but more stringent treatment. Chapuys, while encouraging her to remain firm, urged upon her the need to be more tactful and the advisability, for her own good, of not annoying the King any more than she could help.

The next time she heard they were to move, her sense of insecurity was such that she sent to Chapuys three times in less than twenty-four hours to ask what she should do. As a result of his calming advice, she behaved in such a way that her natural sweetness of character obtained for her much better treatment. She was able to make the journey separately from Elizabeth and allowed to travel in an open barge from Greenwich to Richmond. She saw, and was seen by Chapuys, who had by arrangement stationed himself in a small house overlooking the river Thames. They looked at each other but did not speak or exchange signals. Chapuys reported that she looked to be in good health and appeared to be happy and very cheerful. She was no doubt elated that their little ruse had been successful.

For a long two years, Mary remained in a menial position in Elizabeth's household wherever it happened to be—at Hatfield, at Hunsdon (a Boleyn house), the More, Eltham, Richmond. She was ill-treated and underfed, short of money and in need of clothes. She was under the supervision of Elizabeth's governess, Lady Sheldon, the sister of Anne's father. Lady Sheldon showed some pity for the panic-stricken girl in her care and did not always carry out to the letter the severe measures laid down by Anne. When the Duke of Norfolk and Lady Rochford remonstrated with her for being too kind to the "bastard," she replied that Mary deserved good treatment because of her goodness and virtue. Even so, she could show little lenience, and Mary's state of wretchedness was not much alleviated.

Mary was, however, able to continue her studies in a modified way. Dr. Fetherstone visited her on at least one occasion, although he was no longer her schoolmaster.

A further act of spite was to deprive Mary of some of the consolations of her religion by sending away her confessor and replacing him with a Lutheran. The maid whose job it was to taste her food was also sent away. There was a rumor that Anne was going to have Mary poisoned. Lady Sheldon was horrified when she heard it, for she realized that she would be held responsible if anything happened to the girl in her care. Both Katharine and Chapuys feared that some of Mary's digestive upsets might be due to poisoning as well as depression and misery. Her sufferings were also too serious to be explained by her usual ailment, "her old guest"* as she and, later on, Elizabeth called it. The King was concerned enough to allow Katharine to send her doctor when he was not too busy attending to her own health. He also sent his personal physician, Dr. Butts. But Henry's mistrust was such that he stipulated three conditions for the doctors: they were first to pay their respects to the Princess Elizabeth; they were only to see Mary in the presence of witnesses; and they were to speak in English. Mary had once managed to transmit a message to the outside world by speaking in Latin to Dr. Fetherstone when no one else present understood the language.

Katharine was emboldened to request, through Chapuys, that Mary should be allowed to stay with her at Kimbolton, where she was then living under close supervision, in order to share "a little comfort and

---

*Mary suffered from amenorrhea. In other words, her periods were non-existent or irregular. Her trouble could have been constitutional, aggravated by the stress she underwent in puberty, but, whatever the cause, the so-called cure of "bleeding" did nothing to help her. Mary was to have menstrual difficulties all her life.

mirth." Henry cared about the state of Mary's health, but not enough to take the risk of her being carried out of England by her friends. He did not trust Katharine, but she understood his fears. She offered to stand surety for Mary's continued presence with her own life, adding that as far as she was concerned it was her determination to die in this country. Henry refused her request and expressed his annoyance that Mary should choose to be obedient to her mother rather than her father.

Mary recovered but was still closely guarded, as Henry knew there was a real danger of her being abducted. She knew that her life was in danger and was very frightened. Chapuys was able to send one of his servants to ask her if she would like to escape to Europe, to which she replied that she desired nothing else. He made plans for seizing Mary and putting her on board ship, but the risks and dangers proved to be too great and the plans had to be abandoned.

Anne's own position had changed meanwhile, and was no longer so secure as it had been. The fascination she had exercised over Henry was waning and his amorous attentions were wandering. Mary's treatment alternated between strict repression and spells of comparative freedom when she was allowed to see people and move around—partly depending on the state of Anne's relationship with Henry at the time and partly on Henry's fears of what action the Emperor had in mind in regard to protecting the interests of his aunt and cousin. It was always a possibility that he might invade. But Anne became pregnant again and the hope that she would this time produce the much-desired son kept Henry, if not faithful, at any rate more susceptible to her whims.

By the end of 1535, Henry was threatening that during the next session of Parliament a means would be found to get rid of his first family. But Katharine's health was rapidly deteriorating without need of outside assistance to bring her life to its conclusion. Chapuys obtained permission to make one last visit, but he was not able to obtain the same privilege for Mary when she asked him to intercede with the King on her behalf. Katharine died on January 7, 1536, shortly before her daughter's twentieth birthday. Mary was not told of her death until four days later, nor was she allowed to attend the funeral service in Peterborough on January 21 when Katharine was buried as the Princess Dowager, widow of Prince Arthur. Mary's place as chief mourner was taken by Eleanor, second daughter of the King's sister Mary. Henry and Anne were overjoyed at the news of Katharine's death, of which they felt was a cause for celebration, not sorrow. And during the festivities Henry carried his little daughter Elizabeth about in his arms as he had long ago carried Mary.

Mary's extreme distress again caused her to become very ill. Chapuys thought she would die of grief. Her condition was not improved by the unconfirmed rumor that Katharine had been poisoned. She believed it, as did the Emperor, and feared that the same fate was in store for her. Katharine, whose possessions at the end had been so few, had asked that Mary should be given a gold collar she had brought with her from Spain and some of the furs from her robes. Mary was not permitted to receive these gifts, however, unless she showed signs of obedience to her father, which she felt unable to do. Cromwell went so far as to demand that she should give up a small cross of little real worth but of great sentimental value to her because it had been a gift from her mother. No act was too petty if it could be thought to be effective in breaking her spirit.

Henry was once again awaiting the birth of a son. Anne took advantage of the situation to exercise any influence still left to her. But Mary found her own sense of loneliness and uncertainty as hard to bear as Anne's little acts of tyranny. She had never been very sure of herself. Now, with no mother, an unfriendly father and an atmosphere of impending change, she knew less than ever what to expect or what to do. The only person she could depend on was not so much her kinsman the Emperor, who was too far away and impersonal, but his representative Chapuys, whom she was forbidden to see. His advice could only come by letter or through his servants. And, as the situation was different with Katharine dead, his advice changed too.

Realizing that Mary's life could still be in danger, Chapuys urged her not to enter into any arguments with the King's messengers. He thought that it should not be too difficult for her now to recognize Anne as Queen without casting doubts on her mother's former status as such, and it might help her evade a number of problems. Again it seemed a good idea that she should leave the country. Mary could not have agreed more. She had dramatic notions of drugging the women around her, creeping past her governess's window and quietly letting herself out of the gate at dead of night. Even if she had been successful in those maneuvers, there still remained the problem of getting her on board a ship and, once she was on board, getting the ship safely out of English waters. As she was not always kept in the same house, and was not always therefore the same distance from the river, the problem was even greater. Chapuys, realizing that he would be blamed if she were successful in getting away, made arrangements for an alternate ambassador to take over while the escape was taking place. His alternate arrived but Chapuys did not leave, for the plan, as before, was too dangerous to be feasible.

In the meantime, Anne had miscarried. She realized then that everything was over for her as Queen. Henry was in love with Jane Seymour, one of her own

THE LADY MARY • 45

maids of honor. The situation was repeating itself, but this time she was the wife to be discarded because she could not bear him a son. Henry's methods of getting rid of Anne were no less dishonorable than those he had used to rid himself of Katharine, but they were different and decidedly quicker. His first decision, to divorce Anne, was welcomed by practically everybody. What followed shocked the whole of England. On May 2, Anne was arrested and sent to the Tower. Charges of incest and adultery were brought against her. On May 17, her marriage was declared null and void and, by implication, Elizabeth a bastard (the name by which Chapuys always referred to her). Again Henry did not seem to be troubled by his own lack of logic: if Anne had never been his wife she could not be accused of adultery. Two days later she was beheaded. On May 20, Henry and Jane Seymour were betrothed, and ten days afterward they were married.

It has been said that while Anne was in the Tower and knew the end was near she repented of her treatment of Mary and sent to ask forgiveness. Whether the story is true or not, Mary's charity was such that she could pray that the Lord in his great mercy would forgive Anne. But the King had no tender feelings left for the woman he had once loved so dearly that he had been willing to deny the Pope for her sake. He told his son the Duke of Richmond "that both he and his sister, meaning the Princess, ought to thank God for having escaped from the hands of that woman, who had planned their death by poison."[6]

Henry now had three children he recognized as his and all of them he considered to be illegitimate. Mary still had the best chance of succeeding him if he did not produce a son by his legitimate wife—for Jane was his first Queen whose status could not possibly be questioned. But Henry was still optimistic. Although he

*Jane Seymour, third Queen of Henry VIII. Died October 1537, shortly after giving birth to Edward, Henry's only legitimate son. (Hans Holbein.)* MAURITS HUIS, THE HAGUE.

was forty-five—gross and heavy, no longer the athletic figure of his youth—he had a wife at least twenty years younger, nearer to Mary's age than his own.* Mary was not so much concerned about her rights of succession as about her father's state of grace. When it was a question of which of his marriages was legal, to her mother or to Anne, she cared a great deal; when it was a question of religion, of denying the Pope and, according to her belief, risking his soul, she cared at least as much. But the thought of a male heir who would take away her own chance of succession did not seem to disturb her at all. Similarly, Jane seemed to be less concerned about the succession of her future children than with Mary's well-being. She urged Henry to recognize Mary as his heir again and was told in reply not to be such a fool as to prejudice the rights of any children she might bear to him.

## 2. Reconciliation

The future looked brighter for Mary than it had for nine years. Chapuys approved of the Seymour alliance on two counts: Jane was well disposed toward Mary and, being of the same faith, could be a means of attracting Henry back into the hands of the Roman Church. The Emperor hopefully offered to mediate between the English King and the Pope, but his offer was not accepted. Henry had his own pride and obstinacy. He was neither prepared to go back on his own actions nor to accept a disobedient daughter back into his good graces, in spite of Jane's attempts at persuasion.

---

*Jane's age at the time of her marriage has been variously estimated to have been twenty-five and nineteen.

Once people thought it safe to show their feelings, there was great enthusiasm for Mary. She herself felt encouraged to send a letter to Cromwell (not to Henry directly) to ask him to obtain permission for her to write to her father. Her first letter, dated May 26, was signed, "Your loving friend, Mary." In it, she apologized for her "evil writing," as she had written no letters for two years. She had an uphill task ahead of her. A series of letters followed, both to her father and to Cromwell, in which she became progressively more contrite and more abject. Nothing she wrote of her own free will was sufficient to satisfy Henry. Eventually she copied letters drafted for her by Cromwell, who knew what his master expected. He had become for Mary the strong figure on whom she had to lean. When Henry accepted that she should be allowed to write to him, he did not deign to reply to his "most humble daughter and handmaid," as she signed herself. He wanted not contrition but an acceptance of all the terms he had tried to force upon her during her mother's lifetime. This was more than Mary could bring herself to do of her own volition. She was able to write for herself that she would put herself entirely at Henry's mercy *next to Almighty God*, but this was not enough.

The more she wrote and the more she worried, the worse Mary felt. "The pain in my head and teeth hath troubled me so sore these two or three days, and doth yet so continue, that I have very small rest, day or night."[7] A document admitting her own illegitimacy was brought for her to sign. She still had enough strength, or obstinacy, to refuse. Henry was angry. If possible, Cromwell was even more so because he was afraid that, if he was unsuccessful in bringing Mary to her knees, his own life would be in danger. The Duke of Norfolk and other nobles again came to persuade Mary to accept the King's will. When she still showed herself adamant they lost their tempers and said, if she were their daughter "they would beat her and knock her head so violently against the wall, that they would make it soft as baked apples."[8]

Back Mary went to Chapuys for advice. He said she should accept the King's terms if she felt her life to be in danger. She had to face death not only for herself but also for her friends who were suspected of bolstering her courage. The King's Council deliberated over Mary's case for a week—while Cromwell lived in fear. His fate rested in her hands. In the end the Council decided that another document should be sent for her to sign before they decided on what punishment she should receive if she refused. This time, Mary signed without reading what was put in front of her, though Chapuys said she was already aware of its contents. (Mary was so nearsighted that she could only read by holding the paper close to her eyes. She probably preferred, therefore, to scrutinize important documents in private first.) In so doing, Mary swore to accept Henry as Supreme Head of the Church of England; she denied the authority of the Pope; and perhaps hardest of all (for the particular must have been harder to bear than the general), she admitted that her mother's marriage to her father had not been valid and therefore she was not legitimate. Having accepted all that she had spent so many years in refuting, she immediately asked Chapuys to obtain for her a secret dispensation from the Pope for having done so. Chapuys, in order to comfort her, assured her that "God regarded more the intention than the act."

Some people have said that Mary was to blame for violating her own conscience. But the question arises as to whether it was entirely a matter of her own conscience. She was extremely susceptible to advice from people she trusted and obstinate in carrying out

*Henry VIII in his early forties. (After Hans Holbein, c. 1536 )*
NATIONAL PORTRAIT GALLERY, LONDON.

that advice. As long as her mother was alive she had depended on her and had behaved according to her counsel. Neither had she wanted to do anything that could contribute to her mother's already overflowing cup of grief. On this occasion, however, the Emperor, through Chapuys, and her new friend Cromwell ("I take you for one of my closest friends," she had written) had encouraged her to submit. The Emperor, whom she believed had her interests at heart, was really quite cynical in his motives. Friendship with England was important to him at this juncture and he could ill afford time or money to come to Mary's active defense. Katharine's death had relieved him of the immediate necessity of upholding the Pope's decision on the validity of her marriage.

    With hindsight, it would seem that both Katharine and Mary would have done better for themselves in the worldly sense if they had given in to Henry's demands at the beginning. Each was protecting the interests of the other. It is tempting to speculate on what might have happened if they had behaved differently. Their lives would certainly have been passed in comparative peace and comfort; their mental and physical health would have been much better. Even if Mary had only found herself able to respond to Anne's occasional apparent overtures of friendship she would have found her physical conditions of living much eased. Anne's anger and temper flared because she felt that she was always rudely rebuffed by Katharine and Mary. On a wider scale, Henry would not have had cause to repudiate the Pope; the lives of famous men like Fisher and More would have been spared, as well as the lives of many less well-known. Cromwell and Cranmer would have met with greater difficulties in carrying out their Protestant reforms so that the Reformation would have taken many more years to come into effect.

At first Mary was depressed at the thought of what she had done to gain her father's good will. But when she received a letter from him containing his blessing, and Cromwell and the other messengers who brought it knelt to ask her pardon, she became cheerful and happy. She was especially pleased with Cromwell's expressions of good will. She believed her troubles to be over and was no doubt not averse to the thought that the life of privilege to which she had formerly been accustomed was about to begin again. The nation, generally speaking, rejoiced at the expectation of having their Princess restored to them, hoping too that her return to favor would bring back the old state of affairs existing before Anne had become Queen. It had taken just over two weeks from the date of her first letter to Cromwell for her submission to become acceptable. Even then, she had to follow it up with a lengthy letter to her father spelling out in full the confession of her sins. She ended by praying God to send him and his Queen a child. This may have been more than a conventional wish to please her father, for it would mean that she could live quietly with her own household. She no longer had the strength to fight for the succession and, as she often repeated, she had no desire whatsoever to marry.

At the end of the first week in July, the King and Queen made a secret visit to Mary. Henry gave her some money "for her little pleasures" and Jane gave her a diamond. There was talk of her returning to court, but no date was mentioned. Henry was affable, but not entirely gracious. He indicated that he had not forgotten her former disobedience. He was also sufficiently disturbed by the signs of her popularity in the country to hesitate before showing her signs of favor which he might regret. He did not want to encourage the discon-

tented in his realm to rally to her against him; and he did
not want to reinstate her if he might have to contradict
himself when, and if, Jane bore him what he would call
legitimate children. So he resisted pressure by foreign
powers to have her recognized. To them it was important that there should be no ambiguity about her birth if
she were to be betrothed to one of their princes. But
Henry was content to encourage France against the Emperor, and vice versa, while he played for time. Besides,
there was still the Duke of Richmond, whose accession
was a possibility which would affect Mary's future.

There was, therefore, a period of transition when
nobody quite knew what the situation was or how to
behave. Mary and Elizabeth were still sharing the same
house at Hunsdon. At first the Sheldons continued to
run it and Lady Margaret Bryan (Mary's former nurse)
looked after Elizabeth. She wrote to Cromwell to beg
him to have Elizabeth's welfare at heart and to look after
her needs. She was puzzled, she said, as she had no
instructions, only hearsay, as to the new status of her
charge, who was also badly in need of new clothes—
having presumably grown out of her old ones. Mary, as
part of her submission, had had to write to Cromwell to
say she was willing to call "Princess" the child she had
formerly refused to call anything but "sister," though in
fact Elizabeth had been made illegitimate by law on July
8 and was to be known as the Lady Elizabeth. Cromwell
started to show favor to Mary. He sent her a present of a
horse for which she was most grateful. He gave her the
title of Princess until he realized that he had been a little
premature in so doing and immediately stopped. Chapuys rationalized the problem for Mary by saying it did
not matter which title was used as it had never been
customary to give the name of Princess of Wales to
daughters when there was a possibility of male issue. It

would seem that everybody was waiting to see if Jane could produce the son who would settle the succession once and for all.

Gradually, the positions of Mary and Elizabeth were reversed. Mary was given an allowance, though not a very big one. She even had the courage a little later on to ask for it to be increased. Her establishment was enlarged to comprise forty-two people, not so many as at New Hall but sizeable compared with what she had had for the last two years. Elizabeth's was smaller and subservient to her sister's. Elizabeth became the neglected one though not by Mary, who not only gave her many presents but interceded for her with the King. Mary's privy purse accounts[9] begin at the end of 1536 and are most interesting for the light they shed on her character and way of life. She traveled a great deal. She paid money constantly to her doctor and apothecary, very often for blood-letting, a fashionable remedy for many ills in those days. She gave and received endless presents—she gave to relatives, friends, godchildren and to those for whom she felt pity; she tipped servants and tradesmen who rendered services or who brought her items such as strawberries, oranges, a swan, a pheasant, cheese. She also spent considerable sums of money on gambling at cards.

On July 22, the Duke of Richmond died of tuberculosis, thereby removing one obstacle to Mary's succession. Henry reconsidered her position with the result that on August 30, she was proclaimed heiress-apparent in a London church, though not by act of Parliament. Henry was still appearing to contemplate seriously betrothals between Mary and a candidate put up by Charles on the one hand and the Duke of Orleans again on the other. But the likelihood of her being able to marry a foreigner and live abroad was out of the question if she was heir to the throne.

Mary still had not been allowed back at court. Henry showed no signs of making her legitimate, which would have been possible if he had admitted that she had been conceived in good faith: that he and Katharine were not aware at that time that their marriage was not valid. Other events in the kingdom also occupied Henry's attention and put Mary back into a position of considerable danger, although she was completely innocent. The north and east rose up in rebellion against the King, but swore to be true to his "lawful issue"—which could only be interpreted as Mary at that time. The *Pilgrimage of Grace*, as the uprising was called, was the culmination of a long feeling of unrest and dissatisfaction caused by the many measures enacted since the fall of Wolsey. The dissolution of the smaller monasteries by Cromwell was the spark that ignited the fire that had been smouldering all these years. Cromwell had had his training in Wolsey's attempts to reform the church, but he and Cranmer in their zeal had gone much further. They had taken advantage of Henry's predicament vis-à-vis Katharine to take away not only the authority of the Pope but also the power and the wealth and the ceremonial of the established Church in England. Not everybody was in agreement. There was a growing body of Protestant belief both among the learned and the ignorant, but there was an even stronger element of conservative opinion which had kept silent only because suppressed and afraid of the consequences if it dared to voice its disapproval. They were the advocates of Katharine and Mary, some of whom had even urged that Charles should come to the aid of his aunt and cousin with an army—an invitation he was not eager to accept.

Cromwell and Henry's loyal supporters suppressed the rebellion by treachery and cruelty. The King encouraged "dreadful execution upon a good number of the inhabitants, hanging them on trees, quartering them and setting their heads and quarters in every town, as shall be a fearful warning."[10] The Duke of Norfolk said proudly that so great a number had never been put to death at one time before. Mary herself had taken no part in the rebellion, neither by active encouragement nor by tacit consent. But Henry's fears that his apparently submissive daughter could become the focal point of a political uprising had been realized. Thereafter, a closer watch was kept on her movements and Henry showed no desire to make any change in her status. On the contrary, her total subjugation to his authority was emphasized. She was made to send letters to the Queen of Hungary (the Emperor's sister and Mary's cousin, acting Regent of the Netherlands) and to the Pope admitting that she recognized the invalidity of her parents' marriage and her own illegitimacy. Chapuys told the Emperor that her life would have been in danger if she had not complied. But, as before, secret documents were prepared to salve her conscience and safeguard her future. And the Pope was encouraged to absolve her from her admission by issuing a blanket forgiveness for all those who had fallen into "the new English errors."

Sometime during the following year, Mary is known to have come to court to visit the Queen, who was pregnant. On October 12, 1537, Jane gave birth to a son. The child lived but the mother died. At last, after three marriages covering a period of twenty-eight years, Henry had an heir to whom no one could deny the legal right of succession. Mary was tacitly relegated to second place. The prince was christened Edward in the chapel of Hampton Court, and Mary was one of his godmothers. Both Henry's daughters had places of honor at the ceremony and the four-year-old Elizabeth held Mary's hand as they walked back to the palace. The Queen was buried at Windsor Castle with solemn pomp. Mary was chief mourner. History cannot tell us whether she offered a prayer and shed a tear in memory of her own mother whose simpler funeral, eighteen months earlier, she had not been allowed to attend.

Henry and his Council sometimes allowed Mary such semblances of liberty and honor, which served both to placate the Emperor and to mislead the English people as to her real status. Generally, however, she was confined to her own residence. She was aware of the danger she would run if she overstepped the rules of conduct laid down for her, which she knew existed although she was not sure of their nature. She had learned to be cautious. She spent her time in reading and studying; she played on her musical instruments; she talked to her ladies-in-waiting; and she played cards. Her household had the reputation of virtue and goodness lacking at court, but even so she managed to arouse suspicion in those who watched her. On one occasion, she had to write a letter of apology to Sir Cromwell (as Chapuys called him, for he had recently been knighted) for having allowed what had been considered unsuitable guests to stay in her house. Henry was afraid that his enemies at home might try to make use of Mary and that she, only too conscious of his callous treatment of her, might be amenable to their persuasions. He did not realize that his daughter had the integrity he lacked; that she was not motivated by ambition, her principal desire only being to have his affection and good will.

The Emperor's envoys were aware of the confined nature of her life when they visited her. They asked her if she would like to leave the country. This time she did not answer affirmatively, as she had on a previous occasion. She hesitated, and then said she still hoped that her father's attitude to her would change. She added that only if her life were again in danger would she like to reconsider. She must have preferred to live in England, the only country she had ever known, if only her father would show himself well disposed toward her. But Henry showed no signs of forgiveness or fatherly love. Six months after Jane's death, when court mourning should have been over, he was asked on Mary's behalf what she should wear. He indicated that it did not matter to him what she wore. But it mattered to Mary. She liked fine clothes—a harmless worldly trait which seems out of character but endearing in this otherwise austere young woman—but she did not want to do anything that might irritate her father.

Possible bridegrooms were still being discussed for Mary even though she carried the stain of illegitimacy. When seeking friendship with the French King, Henry seemed to welcome the idea that Mary should marry his son. When wishing to appear to conciliate the Emperor, whose wife had just died, he had the effrontery to suggest, though it is difficult to believe he was serious, that Charles should marry Mary and Charles's son Philip should marry Elizabeth. The fact that Charles had once repudiated his betrothal to Mary when she was a child was not mentioned. It is likely that Mary would not have been displeased with this plan. To have married an older man who was at the same time the relative on whom she had always relied would have eased many of her worries.

But Charles had plenty of problems of his own. The Empire for the sake of which he had staked so much in his youth had never been cohesive, and he had a continual struggle to maintain his sovereignty over his widespread lands. Spain owed him allegiance as the grandson of Isabella and Ferdinand but was not over-ready to support his expensive campaigns. Although vast riches were being brought back from the newly discovered western hemisphere, Charles could not demand them as his own right. There were many expenses and many claimants to be satisfied. He also had religious problems caused by Luther and his followers. The German princes in his empire paid him little more than lip-service. They were divided among themselves into Protestants and Catholics struggling for power. Both factions were only too ready to rebel or to conspire against their distant Emperor, to take advantage of his preoccupations with other parts of his Empire or with foreign enemies.

Cromwell saw several advantages in making an alliance with the German Protestants. Charles and Francis had just signed a ten-year truce. This alliance would have to be counter-balanced—and what could be better than an English alliance with the dissident part of Charles's empire? If he could persuade Henry to marry one of their Protestant princesses, the cause of the reformed church in England would be advanced. And, if Mary were to marry one of their princes, Charles's influence over his cousin would be reduced.

Two years after the death of Jane Seymour, Henry was still single. He had recovered from his genuine grief and was again not averse to the idea of a new young wife who might bear him more sons. But instead of looking for her in his own court, where he had found his last two wives, he was persuaded by Cromwell to consider a marriage with Anne, the reportedly beautiful sister of the young Duke of Cleves. The Duke's religious beliefs were as ambivalent as Henry's. He did not like the Pope and he did not like Luther. He was therefore open to Cromwell's persuasion and to Henry's. The Duke was also suggested as a husband for Mary (who would thereby have become her stepmother's sister-in-law)—a match that was no more seriously considered by Henry than any other that had been proposed on her behalf.

*Anne of Cleves, fourth Queen of Henry VIII. Marriage annulled six months after it took place but she continued to live in England. (Engraving after Hans Holbein.)* NATIONAL PORTRAIT GALLERY, LONDON.

A perhaps more suitable candidate for her hand was found in another German, the Duke of Bavaria. Arrangements went so far as to have a draft treaty of marriage drawn up and Mary was consulted as to her wishes: in other words, it was clearly indicated to her that here was a choice already made for her by her father and his advisers. She trod carefully. She said that, although she preferred not to embrace the Protestant religion and would rather remain single, she would nevertheless submit to whatever her father thought best. "In this and all other things during my life [he] shall find me his most humble and obedient daughter, subject and servant."[11] The Duke came to visit Mary and declared his willingness to marry her, in spite of some reservations about her illegitimate status. She cautiously agreed to obey her father. In fact, the Duke had more Catholic tendencies than Protestant, but any deviation from her own form of religion was in fact unacceptable to her.

There was no haste to carry out this plan either. Only Cromwell's schemes on Henry's behalf went ahead without hindrance. At the end of 1539 Anne of Cleves, then in her mid-twenties, arrived in England. When Henry first saw her, on January 1, he had a rude shock. She was not the beauty he had been led to expect, and certainly not a woman he had any enthusiasm to marry. But to have cancelled the wedding at that late date would have meant losing face in Europe and alienating the very people whose friendship he was seeking. The arrangements were therefore allowed to go ahead. Henry and Anne were married on January 6, with Mary and Elizabeth both taking part in the ceremony. Six months later there was an amicable arrangement between the King and his new wife to separate. The marriage was annulled on the grounds that she had formerly been betrothed to the Duke of Lorraine and that her marriage to Henry had never been consummated. (Henry was making doubly sure.) The honor of her family was satisfied by the settlement Henry made upon her. Meanwhile, the truce between Charles and Francis had lapsed and with it the need for an Anglo-German alliance.

Anne no doubt found her bridegroom equally repulsive on first sight and the new arrangements not displeasing. She was given a good income, a fine establishment, and two princely houses and she ranked next after the King's children so long as she stayed in England. She had the good sense to make the best of her lot and lived serenely till she died a natural death in 1557. Perhaps surprisingly after such an inauspicious beginning, she managed to retain the King's friendship and was treated and referred to as his sister. She also had a good relationship with Mary, who was only a few months younger than she, and with Elizabeth.

Cromwell was not to be so fortunate. His error not only aroused Henry's anger; it also gave his enemies the opportunity they had been seeking. But first there was a respite while Cromwell did everything in his power to rectify the situation and seemed to be succeeding. While he was trying to undo the marriage he had arranged, he was rewarded, in May, by being made Earl of Essex and a Knight of the Garter. But Henry only supported Cromwell as long as he was useful to him. He had never really gone along with his extreme Protestant views. When Cromwell's Catholic adversaries went into action, Henry made no move to save him.

The Duke of Norfolk and Bishop Gardiner, first accused Cromwell and his fellow Councillor, Sir Richard Rich, of taking bribes. Rich put all the blame on Cromwell. Henry gave permission to the denigrators of his first minister to act. On June 10, during the course of a Council meeting, Norfolk suddenly stood up and denounced Cromwell as a traitor. With pleasure he then tore off the insignia of Cromwell's latest honors, called in the guards already waiting at the door, and dispatched him to the Tower. Nobody who witnessed this scene raised a voice of protest. Cromwell had no further opportunity to see the King and put his case before him. His goods and valuables were seized and taken to the King's Treasury, and he was stripped of all his titles and offices. According to Marillac, the French ambassador, Henry accused him of having wanted to establish the Lutheran church in England contrary to the wishes of the King and Parliament. A week after his arrest, a Bill of Attainder was brought in which stressed the low and base origins from which he had been raised by the King to become his most trusty counsellor only to turn into a traitor. When he had completed his last useful act for Henry—a statement ensuring the annulment of the marriage to Anne of Cleves—he was executed without trial on July 28, 1540.

The Protestant Archbishop of Canterbury, probably Cromwell's only friend other than the King, for excessive power had brought him only enemies, was in a predicament. His own position was in jeopardy if he put a foot wrong. He wrote a letter which was a masterpiece in the circumstances and was accepted by Henry. Cranmer did not deny his friendship but qualified it. "I loved him as my friend, for so I took him to be, but I chiefly loved him for the love which I thought I saw him bear ever toward Your Grace...."[12] He sought to appease the King still further by saying diplomatically that as a loyal subject he was glad that Cromwell's treason had been discovered. An attempt was made to compromise Cranmer and have him also sent to the Tower, but it was frustrated by Henry.

The Duke of Norfolk and several other members of the Privy Council openly rejoiced in Cromwell's downfall, which they had connived to bring about. In an earlier day, Norfolk had protected and recommended him to the King, both before and after Wolsey's downfall, but since that time his protégé had become his rival whom he never failed to regard as an upstart.

Mary said nothing about the fate of the man who had acted as her intermediary with the King and whom she had called friend when she was in distress. Silence was her best ally. But it was said that Cromwell had discouraged all projected marriages for Mary because he had intended to marry her himself in the hope of becoming King. It is not beyond belief that the thought had crossed his mind. For a man who was an unknown commoner by birth to have become son-in-law to the King would have been no mean feat in Tudor times. Cromwell would not only have advanced himself and helped secure his future authority, but would have effectively undermined Mary's position as a leading Catholic. His considerable effort to reconcile father and daughter and to restore Mary to her legitimate status would then appear in a different light: not as a sign of unaccustomed human kindness but one of overweening ambition. He had already shown that he was not unaware of the possible value of strategic marriages when he had married his son to Jane Seymour's sister Elizabeth.

Ten days after his official separation from Anne of Cleves, Henry married Katharine Howard, the pretty nineteen-year-old niece of the Duke of Norfolk, who had deliberately brought them together. In order to increase his already considerable prestige and influence in the kingdom, the Duke had already successfully helped to arrange several royal matches for his family. His daughter Mary had married Henry's natural son, the Duke of Richmond, though this scheme had been frustrated by the latter's early death. It was said that the Duke too had planned to make the Lady Mary his wife. It was perhaps more to be expected of him than of Cromwell that he should have such ideas. His family was already illustrious and powerful. His antecedents could be traced back for centuries. He was the third Duke, and by his first marriage claimed the King as his nephew. He was not warned by the fate of his other niece, Ann Boleyn, nor by the fall of Cromwell, whom he regarded as a mere nobody. He overlooked the flirtatious nature of his niece and ignored the reputation she had already achieved before she married.

The new bride was not content with her old husband, even if he was King of England. She did not consider the consequences of her actions nor the fact that her uncle's enemies would be watching out for any mistakes she might make. She overestimated the power of her new position. She also complained that Mary did not treat her with respect—probably with some justification, as there can have been little compatibility between the two. Nevertheless, Mary did not do anything that might offend her father if she could help it. She sent his fifth Queen a New Year's gift which was accepted with pleasure. (At the same time she also gave her little half-sister a yellow satin kirtle made with five yards of satin.) She did not, however, come to court until May 1541, when Henry insisted upon her presence.

Katharine's royal career was cut ignominiously short before she had been married eighteen months. Significantly, it was Cranmer who informed the King of his wife's supposed infidelities, in an attempt to halt the swing back to Catholicism after the fall of Cromwell. We are told that Cranmer obtained his evidence from one of

*Katherine Howard, fifth Queen of Henry VIII, cousin of Anne Boleyn. Beheaded February 1542. (Identity doubtful. Artist unknown, c. 1541.)*
NATIONAL PORTRAIT GALLERY, LONDON.

the attendants of the old Duchess of Norfolk, with whom Katharine had lived as a girl. This piece of information sheds an interesting light on the kind of spying which went on continually. No one of importance was free from this danger, whether it was the King's wife, the King's daughter or the King's ministers. Although Katharine denied some of the charges brought against her and gained for herself a little time, in the end the evidence was too damning. Henry had no mercy. She followed in the footsteps of her cousin and was executed in February 1542.

Mary's nature was such that she would have felt compassion for this stepmother too if she had been fully aware of what happened. But the shock of other deaths ordered by Henry had reduced her to such a state of physical collapse that Chapuys thought she would not survive. In May 1541, the Countess of Salisbury had been beheaded in a more than usually cruel way. Mary's old godmother, governess and lifelong friend had been sent to the Tower two years earlier, together with other Catholics, as an act of reprisal and vengeance on Henry's part for the behavior of her son, Reginald Pole.

Just after Wolsey's downfall, at a time when the whole family was in favor, Reginald Pole had been offered the Archbishopric of York. But Pole felt very deeply about Henry's attempts to have his marriage to Katharine of Aragon annulled and had let Henry know that neither on religious nor on personal grounds could he support him. He had asked instead for permission to leave the country which, fortunately when one considers what happened to those of similar persuasion such as More and Fisher, was granted. He went to Rome and eventually became a Cardinal. He had remained, however, a constant irritation to Henry. He had spoken publicly against Henry's renunciation of the Pope. He

*Henry VIII toward the end of his life. (Artist unknown, c. 1542.)*
NATIONAL PORTRAIT GALLERY, LONDON.

had been ready to raise help on the continent for the rebels in the *Pilgrimage of Grace*. Two years later he had again tried to muster support for a movement against "the most cruel and abominable tyrant, the King of England."

As Pole was beyond his reach, Henry took his vengeance on the members of the family living in England and on their Catholic friends, past supporters of the cause of Katharine of Aragon and of Mary. During the course of 1538 and 1539 he had sent to the Tower Pole's mother, the Countess of Salisbury; Pole's eldest brother Henry with his son; the Marquess of Exeter with his son Edward Courtenay; and Sir Edward Neville. Henry Pole and Neville were summarily executed. Henry's son was never heard of again. Edward Courtenay was kept in the Tower and educated there. Mary's schoolmaster Fetherstone and her mother's chaplain Thomas Abel, who had been imprisoned for some five years, were also executed. After two years of strict and uncomfortable confinement, the Countess of Salisbury was suddenly, for no good reason, condemned to death, "or rather to eternal life" as Reginald Pole expressed it when he heard the news. In this way Henry rid himself of virtually the last remnants of the Yorkist line.

It is not clear why Mary was persuaded to come to court in May 1541, the month when the Countess of Salisbury was executed. Mary herself was not in the King's good books at the time when he was punishing her friends in so drastic a way—especially as a letter was discovered which supposedly proved that the Pole family had plans to renew an old idea that Mary should marry Reginald Pole. Henry may have been keeping his daughter under even closer supervision than usual, or he may have had a guilty feeling of compassion for her when he saw how ill she had become as a result of recent events. In order to protect her, Chapuys advised the Emperor not to call Henry "uncle" nor to refer to Mary as "Princess," both terms likely to provoke Henry still more.

During the period of Katharine Howard's disgrace, Mary was again moved from court and lived with her cousin Margaret Douglas and the young widow of the Duke of Richmond. The two younger children, Edward and Elizabeth, shared a household and were educated together. For practically a year Mary was seriously ill. Not till the end of May 1542 was Chapuys able to report any improvement. Then he said that at last there was hope that she would soon recover completely "owing to the good diet prescribed by her physicians and the great care her own father and her own servants take of her."[13] Chapuys himself took no small part in trying to cheer and comfort her and Mary was duly appreciative.

A change in Henry's attitude must also have contributed to Mary's peace of mind. He at last found himself able to speak "the most gracious and amiable words a father could address to his daughter."[14] He gave her valuable jewels and a present which must have given her particular pleasure: a book of gold that opened to show miniatures of himself and Katharine of Aragon. Mary appeared at court willingly and took part in the Christmas festivities. She was treated with honor and respect by her father and by everyone else.

Henry's marriage to Katharine Parr in 1543, at which Mary was present, was responsible in part for the maintenance of this change in his behavior. For the rest of her father's life Mary was to enjoy a life of favor and tranquillity and to receive an intellectual and religious stimulus such as had never been her lot before during her adult life, and was never to be again. Although still

KATHARINE PARRE

*Katharine Parr, sixth and last Queen of Henry VIII. After his death married Thomas Seymour of Sudeley. (Attributed to W. Scrots, c. 1545.)*
NATIONAL PORTRAIT GALLERY, LONDON.

troubled by bad health, both by constitution and as a result of the treatment she had received at the hands of ignorant doctors, Mary on the whole was happy. It is hard to imagine that she had any great love left for the gross, cantankerous man her once-handsome father had become. But her strong sense of duty, not to mention relief at the feeling of comparative security she was enjoying, must have helped overcome any repugnance caused by his physical appearance and stifle memories of his past actions.

It was during this period of calm that Chapuys, the Emperor's ambassador to England for sixteen years, retired. He was crippled with rheumatism and too ill to be useful to Mary anymore. He had been her adviser, friend and support through all her troubles as he had been to Katharine of Aragon, and his mind must have been relieved that he could leave her in such changed circumstances.

## 3. Death of Henry VIII

Henry's sixth and, as it turned out, last wife was a very serious young woman of about thirty. She had already been widowed twice but had no children. She was a very good friend to Mary, who was only about three years younger, and a kind stepmother to Edward and Elizabeth. It is likely that Katharine Parr and Mary had known each other as children, for Katharine's mother had been a lady-in-waiting to Katharine of Aragon (after whom her daughter had probably been named). Indeed, they may have shared the same schoolmaster for part of their education. Mary's banishment from court and isolation, first in Elizabeth's household and then in her own, had necessarily cut her off from her old friends.

Katharine Parr herself had spent much of the same period in the provinces. She had been married first when she was about twelve years old to a man already in his fifties or sixties and then, before she was twenty, to a middle-aged man with two children who encouraged her liking for learning. She had already had experience of life with old husbands and young children. But now both Katharine and Mary had the opportunity to discuss academic questions and the religious problems of the day with people of their own generation. Katharine chose for her attendants similarly minded serious young women whom she and Mary had known as children. Among them were Katharine's sister Lady Herbert, the young Duchess of Suffolk (daughter of Katharine of Aragon's friend Maria Salinas), the Countess of Hertford, and the wife of Dudley, Earl of Lisle.

The friendship between Mary and her step-mother was much encouraged by their joint love of learning, though Katharine tended toward a greater freedom of thought than her conservative friend. Under her influence, Mary translated into English from Latin Erasmus's paraphrase of the Gospel according to St. John which was, after Henry's death, edited and published in a collection of paraphrases. Mary allowed her name to be mentioned in the preface after having been persuaded to do so by Katharine. The opportunity for intellectual companionship and dialogue seems to have overcome any scruples Mary might have had about subscribing to a book which was later to be used by the Reformists.

Both Katharine and Mary were kind and generous to Edward and Elizabeth and their affection was returned. It seemed that at last Henry could live in harmony with all his family, and they with him. Naturally, there were still ambitious troublemakers around, and attempts to discredit Katharine on religious grounds nearly succeeded. They were foiled, however, by Henry's support of his wife. At his time of life, and after his other matrimonial experiences, he valued highly a good-looking intelligent young woman who was faithful to him, nursed him and tended his leg sores which by this time had become very painful. He may also have appreciated having a wife who caused no controversy in the family.

Katharine was a Catholic by birth, but her Humanist upbringing had taught her to think for herself and not to accept without question the dogma of priests. Gradually, like many intellectuals of her day, she began to favor the Protestant point of view based on a Bible which could be read in English and interpreted by the reader. She was not only willing to discuss theology with her husband, but was outspoken in the presence of others who were not so well disposed toward her. But, with the example of Henry's other wives and her experience of two husbands, she was too wise not to comply with any wish of Henry's. She was quick to see when her arguments, religious or otherwise, displeased him and gave them up. As a result of her skill, helped by Henry's increasing physical incapacity and his dependence on her as he grew older, she remained safely married to him until the end of his life, a period of three and a half years. But she may in the end only have been saved from Katharine Howard's fate by Henry's timely death. There were rumors that Henry was planning to get rid of her in order to marry either the young widow of his friend the Duke of Suffolk or the Duchess of Richmond (Norfolk's daughter), the even younger widow of his own illegitimate son.

A few months before Henry's death there was a curious report of an attempt on Mary's life. No details are available so it is not known what political or religious faction was supposed to be at the back of it. If the report is true, with Henry's approaching death suspected by all, it may have been a religious attempt to deny her the succession.

In December 1546, Henry sent for Mary to come to his bedside. He said he was sorry not to have found her a husband (possibly the least of Mary's worries) and begged her to be a mother to the young Prince Edward. Mary was overcome with tears and had to leave. Katharine Parr was summoned next. Henry spoke of her jewels which he wished her to keep, but she also was too tearful to speak. Henry did not see his wife or daughter again. Only Cranmer was present at the end.

Henry VIII died on January 28, 1547. He was survived by two of his six wives, Katharine Parr and Anne of Cleves, and three children. In spite of having asked for his friend the Protestant Archbishop to comfort him in his last moments, Henry died a Catholic. His belief in the religion of his birth was reasserted by his bequest of an annual sum for masses to be said for his soul.

By earlier Acts of Parliament*, Henry had obtained for himself the right to name his successors. In his will he recognized the claims of all three of his children. Edward and his "lawfully begotten" heirs were named first in the line of succession, followed by Mary and her heirs, followed by Elizabeth and her heirs. Mary and Elizabeth were each to receive £3,000 a year as long as they remained unmarried and a dowry if they married with the consent of the Privy Council. (This sum cannot be interpreted in terms of today's currency,

*1536 and 1544

but it was considerable at the time and much larger than either sister had been accustomed to receive or expect.)

No reference was made to the legitimacy of his daughters. Indeed, it is difficult to see how Henry could have done so. Not only would he have had to contradict decisions he himself had made long before, which would have been uncharacteristic, but he would have had to discriminate between the two girls. If Mary was legitimate, Elizabeth was not, and vice versa. With one delicate son and one daughter troubled by chronic ill-health, maybe Henry had foresight enough to see that Elizabeth might be the only one to have the stamina to survive for any length of time. If he faced up to the religious problems, which is doubtful, he may also have felt some qualms about Mary's intransigence.

Henry VIII on his deathbed pointing to Edward VI as his successor. The fallen Pope is in the foreground. In the back row from left to right, Somerset, Northumberland (only known portrait), Bedford, Cranmer. (Artist unknown.) NATIONAL PORTRAIT GALLERY, LONDON.

In the event that none of his children or their heirs survived, the crown was to pass to the descendants of the two daughters of his sister Mary and the Duke of Suffolk, Frances and Eleanor Brandon. Frances, Mary's contemporary and first god-daughter, was now Marchioness of Dorset with three daughters, the Ladies Jane, Katharine, and Mary Grey. The two Scottish descendants of Henry's elder sister Margaret were not mentioned, for it was intended that Edward should eventually marry Mary (later Mary, Queen of Scots); and Lady Margaret Douglas, daughter of Margaret by her second marriage was not eligible as her father was not of royal blood.

# CHAPTER III

# THE KING'S SISTER

On February 20, 1547, Henry's one and only legitimate son was crowned Edward VI, King of England and Ireland and Supreme Head of the Church (the first time the Coronation ceremony had included this title). Though a precocious boy, Edward, at the age of nine, was too young to take upon his fragile shoulders all the duties of a King. Foreseeing this, Henry had named in his will a Council of Regency consisting of sixteen members, some Catholics, some Protestants, but most of them politicians first and foremost. Although Mary had reached years of discretion—she was now thirty-one and second to the King in rank—she was not included in the Council. Neither was Katharine Parr, although she had been made Regent in 1544, when Henry was in France with his army. If Henry had hoped to ensure a system of balance of power until such time as Edward was old enough to take control himself, he would have been mistaken. No body of sixteen men could work without a leader. But Henry had not been expecting an early death when he made his will, though he presumably realized the end was near when he signed it.

There was by the end of Henry's reign a new breed of men at the top from whom he chose his Council. They had gradually come up as the old ones had fallen by the wayside (whether in the course of nature, as was the case with the Duke of Suffolk, or with assistance as with Cromwell). After Cromwell's execution in 1540, Henry had never again entrusted any one man with so much power. Norfolk and, to a lesser extent, Gardiner had benefited for a time by the more conservative Catholic attitude which Henry then took, but by the time he died, they too had lost all their authority. One of Henry's last acts was to strike Gardiner off the Council. Another was to sign a Bill of Attainder against Norfolk and his swashbuckling poet son Henry Howard, Earl of Surrey. Among other errors of judgment, Surrey had been rash enough to announce publicly that his father should be sole Regent when Edward ascended the throne—a claim which could not fail to arouse action by their enemies. The son, at the age of thirty, was executed for high treason* and the father survived only because the King died first. Norfolk's opponents apparently had some compunction about ending his life, but none at all about keeping him safely out of their way in the Tower.

Chief among the new men to become members of the Council were Edward and Thomas Seymour, John Dudley, Richard Rich, Thomas Wriothesley, and William Paget. Edward Seymour, already promoted to be Earl of Hertford and Lord Chamberlain before Henry died, now honored himself with the Dukedom of Somerset, assumed the title of Lord Protector (to which the Council agreed) and virtually took over the func-

---

*On July 9, 1977, some five hundred members of the Howard family assembled in Framlingham Church in Suffolk where his beheaded body is buried "to remember the 'sublime poet,' to celebrate his gifts, to bury his suffering, and to rehallow his tomb." (London *Times* March 14, 1977)

*Edward VI, first Protestant King of England. Reigned 1547-1553. (From the studio of Scrots. c. 1546)* NATIONAL PORTRAIT GALLERY, LONDON.

*Edward Seymour, Earl of Hertford, later Duke of Somerset. Lord Protector of England during early part of reign of Edward VI. Beheaded January 1552. (Identity doubtful. Artist unknown.)* NATIONAL PORTRAIT GALLERY, LONDON.

tions of the Crown. His brother Thomas, equally ambitious but less capable and certainly far less adroit, was created Lord High Admiral and assumed the title of Lord Seymour of Sudeley. Lord Dudley (son of the Dudley who had been the unpopular exhorter of taxes in the reign of Henry VII and the first man to be executed by Henry VIII on his accession), now had been given his stepfather's title of Viscount Lisle in 1542, became Earl of Warwick and Lord Chamberlain. Thomas Wriothesley, formerly Cromwell's secretary, became Earl of Southampton and for a brief time held the office of Lord Chancellor before being succeeded by Richard Rich. Sir William Paget was made Chancellor of the Duchy of Lancaster and Comptroller of the King's Household.

Dissident voices were raised in the Council at such self-awarded promotions, but they were not loud enough to be heard. These men had no sooner assumed their new authority, however, than they began to quarrel among themselves. They were as jealous of each other as they had formerly been of their old rivals. This was particularly true of Warwick, who encouraged the already existing conflict between the two Seymour brothers in the hope of bringing them both down. These were also the men who were to be the cause of so much distress to Mary.

Edward VI, who during his father's lifetime had shown himself to be a highly intelligent boy and an affectionate brother, was under great pressure from his uncles. They assumed the authority, but it was Edward—even though a minor—who had in the last resort to sign the papers. They kept a strict watch over him to ensure that he would not fall under any other influence. If at first he did not think as they did, it was not long before he was persuaded to give that impression. Although Edward had been christened and crowned with

Catholic ritual, his tutors were Protestants, as were his uncles. Under their influence he became England's first Protestant King.

This question of religious belief and practice caused a rift in Edward's relationship with Mary. Edward, brought up as a devout Protestant, could not understand that his sister could have a point of view different from his, and Mary could not believe that he was old enough to have a point of view of his own. There was already a growing gulf between Mary and the Protector, although his wife Anne was well known to her and seemingly a friend. (She had been one of Katharine of Aragon's Ladies-in-Waiting.) The Protector had not got in touch with Mary for several days after the death of her father, and she was highly suspicious of him. François van der Delft, the Imperial Ambassador who had succeeded Chapuys, was doubtful whether she was receiving the income stipulated in her father's will. When he asked Mary, she said she had no way of judging: "The testament which was said to be that of the late King might or might not be genuine; she did not know."[1] She also did not know what had happened to her mother's dowry, though no doubt she could have guessed that it had been spent. It had certainly not been reserved through all her tribulations to form part of her own dowry—as the Emperor and his ambassador appeared to think should have been done.

Mary's attempts to be a "mother" to Edward, as their father had requested, were doomed from the start. She was allowed to give him presents and to visit him from time to time, but the atmosphere at court was not to her liking and her health was so poor that she preferred to stay in her own home. All that fall she was in a state of profound melancholy. After the first Christmas, which Edward, Elizabeth and Mary spent together, she no longer came to court for the festive seasons, or in-

*Thomas Seymour, Baron of Sudeley. Lord High Admiral during early part of reign of Edward VI. Married Katharine Parr after the death of Henry VIII. Beheaded March 1549. (Artist unknown. Painted after Seymour's death.)* NATIONAL PORTRAIT GALLERY, LONDON.

deed for any long period of time. But each year, after Christmas was over, she made a point of visiting her brother. Edward had been in the habit of writing her rather stilted but affectionate letters in Latin. Later, these became rarer and more critical. On one occasion, before his father's death, Edward wrote to Mary, "even so I write to you very rarely, yet I love you most."[2] Four days later he wrote to his stepmother to complain that Mary was too fond of "foreign dances and merriments which do not become a most Christian princess."[3] Considering how remarkably devout, modest and restrained Mary's general behavior was, it is surprising that she should have been taken to task for indulging in one of her rare lighthearted pastimes.

Mary had had experience of not being wanted but was now better able to cope with the situation. She had an independent income and household (although perhaps not as large as she should have had). She retired once more into private life. She was sorry not to see her brother, for she felt it her duty to help him, but she realized that she was powerless to interfere.

For about two years she was left undisturbed. She spent her time, surrounded by her Catholic ladies and friends, in one or another of the houses left her by her father—chiefly in New Hall (her old home in Essex), Kenninghall (formerly belonging to the Duke of Norfolk), and Hunsdon in Herefordshire, where she had spent much time with the young Elizabeth. There were again vague marriage plans for her, but the Council did not pursue them any more than had her father. The same reasons held good: chiefly that they did not want her to leave the country or a foreign bridegroom to come to England.

Mary's friendship with Katharine Parr lapsed, and the intellectual côterie of enlightened young

women formed at court during the period of Henry's
last marriage was dissolved, for Katharine suddenly
showed herself in a different light. The dutiful wife did
not become a sorrowing widow. No sooner was Henry
buried than she and Thomas Seymour were secretly
married. It was said that she had been in love with him
before, but if Henry had suspected that his wife was
unfaithful, the rumor that he was about to get rid of her
would have been based on fact. Thomas Seymour, on
the other hand, would seem to have been more influenced by the thought of a match that might advance his
career than he was by passion. He is said to have unsuc-
cessfully proposed marriage both to the Duchess of
Richmond and to the thirteen-year-old Princess Elizabeth before he married the Queen. After the event,
Seymour deceitfully went through the form of asking
Edward for his approval and Mary to help him in his
suit, as if the marriage had not already taken place. Edward readily consented, noting afterward in his journal
that the marriage much offended Seymour's brother, the
Lord Protector. Mary indicated that the idea did not
please her but that it was not a matter in which she cared
to meddle, "wooing matters set apart, wherein I being a
maid am nothing cunning."[4] She said it was for the
King's widowed Queen to decide whether it was proper
for her to marry again.

Elizabeth was informed after the marriage was
made public in June 1547. In a letter said to have been
sent by her to Mary (the original is not in existence),
she wrote that though she shared her sister's disapproval, she was prepared to dissimulate. It was pointless
to argue, "since neither you nor I, dearest sister, are in
such a condition as to offer any obstacle thereto, without running heavy risk of making our own lot much
worse than it is."[5] She also did not wish to appear un-
grateful to Katharine who had always been so kind to

*Princess Elizabeth, age 13(?) Daughter of Henry VIII and Anne Boleyn. Succeeded her half-sister Mary as Queen of England in 1558. (Artist unknown.)* COPYRIGHT RESERVED.

her. Elizabeth had been left in the care of her stepmother and was living with her in Chelsea (together
with her own large household of over a hundred people). When the marriage was made public, she continued to stay with the Seymours. Thomas Seymour, the
Admiral, paid the Princess more attention than was
proper and "familiarities" were alleged to have taken
place between them which shocked Elizabeth's governess. In September of the following year Katharine died
giving birth to a daughter, the only child she produced
during all her four marriages. By that time Elizabeth had
left them and had a household of her own.

Thomas Seymour was handsome and gallant, obviously able to make himself very attractive to some
women. He was not so popular with the other members of the Council, especially his brother, against
whom he was constantly scheming. He wanted to be in
sole charge of the King, whose good will he attempted
to obtain by giving him presents and extra money. He
had a grand plan for Edward to marry Lady Jane Grey,
the eldest daughter of Frances Brandon, Mary's first
goddaughter (now wife of the Marquis of Dorset) and
granddaughter of Henry VIII's sister Mary.* The intended match between Edward and the infant Mary,
Queen of Scots, had fallen through as she had been
taken to France and betrothed to the Dauphin.

Jane Grey, the same age as Edward, was already
part of Katharine Parr's household and presumably a
younger companion to Elizabeth. It was a common practice for young girls of good family to be sent to court or
into other noble families for their education. Jane was,
in any case, of royal blood and mixed with her cousins
on familiar terms. The Admiral expected to gain more
power if the King should marry his ward. He had no

*See page 5.

trouble in getting Dorset, also moved by ambition, to agree with him. He even persuaded Dorset to sell him the right to Jane's guardianship. But when Katharine Parr died, Jane was summoned home. The Admiral persuaded her parents to allow Jane to come back, with his mother as chaperone, in the hope that his scheme might still be brought to fruition. He may also have been anxious to defeat his brother Edward's plan to marry his own daughter to the King. But the Admiral was suspected of not being averse to marrying Jane himself—if he did not marry Mary—or Elizabeth. The rumors flew. There was a story current in Europe, reported by van der Delft to the Emperor (who had already heard it) that Thomas Seymour had tried to murder the King, that he had intended to murder both Mary and his brother and then marry Elizabeth in order to set himself on the throne.

Somerset was sorely tried by his brother's antics. And Warwick did what he could to widen the breach between them, hoping to profit thereby. Six months after the death of Katharine, Thomas Seymour's position vis-á-vis his nephew had been so successfully undermined that there was no difficulty in convincing the King that a charge of high treason—the favorite indictment for bringing down a political enemy—should be brought against him. The young King recorded his uncle's execution in his journal without comment: "Also the Lord Sudeley, Admiral of England, was condemned to death and died in the March ensuing [1549]."[6] Shortly afterward, Warwick became Lord Admiral.

Under Somerset's Protectorship the reforms of the Church begun in the reign of Henry VIII had been actively continued. Already in 1538 Cranmer's English Bible had been placed in every church in England. Eleven years later, the clergy were forbidden to use any writings whatsoever, whether in English or Latin, which had not been authorized by the King and his advisers. Mass was prohibited and all books connected with it were ordered to be burned. Cranmer's first English prayer book became compulsory. The *Statute of Uniformity* was passed, which imposed increasingly large fines followed by imprisonment on anyone disobeying the new regulations. Gardiner was sent to the Tower for refusing to conform. Later, the Bishops of Chichester and Durham were deprived of their sees. Archbishop Cranmer and the Bishops Latimer, Hooper and Ridley were the leading churchmen at the head of the movement.

The Protestant reforms did not pass without expressions of discontent from the people. There were rebellions in various parts of the country, which had to be put down by force. But there appeared to be some confusion in people's minds as to whether they were rising against the religious reforms or the agrarian reforms which took place at the same time.

Mary was fully aware of the changes taking place in the kingdom and naturally thought they were for the worse. She realized too that the *Statute of Uniformity* could bring her into great trouble. She was, however, by virtue of the Emperor's tutelage as well as by habit, extremely cautious. She did not allow herself to be made use of by dissidents of any persuasion, although she was suspected of doing so. She never faltered in her loyalty to the King, but she was torn by her conflicting loyalty to her faith. Her feeble health could not stand the strain and she was constantly ill. She was again frightened for she did not know what might happen to her. She said she was ready to face death for her beliefs—but it was a fate she would rather avoid.

She sought help from the Emperor and his sister. The Emperor too was well informed about the new Act before it was put into effect on May 1, 1549. He immediately took steps to protect his cousin. Van der Delft was to intercede with Somerset before he could take any irreversible action against Mary, while Charles himself was to talk to the English ambassador, Paget, who was then visiting his court. There were to be no threats, but it was to be made delicately clear that the Emperor would intervene strongly if any attempts were made to compel Mary to conform or if, through fear of maltreatment, she showed any signs of accepting the changes. He need have had no doubts on the latter score: Mary was constant to the faith in which she had been brought up. But she was not satisfied with vague promises of support. She begged the Emperor, in one of her rare letters to him (Van der Delft intermediated between them as a rule) to say more specifically what he would do if she were threatened with violence.

In fact, nobody showed any signs of doing her violence; and Mary, perhaps not surprisingly in view of her past experiences, reacted with unnecessary hysteria. Charles was more concerned about prevention than cure, both for Mary's sake and because he did not want to be called upon to take positive action on her behalf. He still had enough problems of his own. With this in mind, he talked to Paget, who, according to the Emperor's report at the time, said the Council did not intend to apply the new law to Mary. (The Emperor later changed this to say that Paget had actually *promised* not to apply the law, to which the Council replied that he did not have the authority to do so.) At the same time, van der Delft obtained from Somerset verbal assurances that Mary would be allowed to have Mass said privately in her chamber. Charles was not satisfied that her future was sufficiently safeguarded by such a promise, though Mary would have preferred not to press the point. He asked for the dispensation in writing so that neither the

King nor Parliament could ever molest her, directly or indirectly; for, as he said to Paget on another occasion, "We had often seen it happen, particularly in England, that some made laws and others, who came into power afterwards, applied them; and he must not find it strange that we should ask for some further statement and assurance from the English, who had been known to execute their queens."[7]

The Protector's answer was simply that he could not contradict in writing the laws of the realm, but he would give his word that Mary would not be interfered with as long as she practiced her religion in private. It would seem that Somerset was not ill disposed toward Mary and was at first content if she would *seem* to obey the law. But he was pressed hard by the Emperor and exasperated by Mary's stubborn and defensive attitude. "We have not forbidden the Lady Mary to hear Mass privately in her own apartment, but whereas she used to have two Masses said before, she has three said now since the prohibitions, and with greater show."[8] Somerset thought, with some justification from his and the Council's point of view, that Mary should outwardly be strict in observance of the law. As the King's sister and his heir, she should set a good example to the country as a whole. He knew that she was loyal to the King in everything except her religion, but she could easily again become the focal point for dissent on other than religious grounds. If Mary had cooperated from the start and had only heard her Mass in private she would have been in no danger of interference. But this was not in her nature. The more she was frightened, the more aggressive she became in the practice of her religion. So attempts were made to intimidate her.

The Council made its first move in June 1549. The new Chancellor, Lord Rich, and the Secretary, Dr.

Petre, came to see Mary in the hope of converting her and frightening away her priests. Mary was firm in her refusal, as she was to be to all further attempts to persuade or coerce her. Her argument, given to her by the Emperor, was that until her brother was old enough to enforce laws for himself she would remain obedient to the laws of her father.

Later that same year, it seemed as if the Protector might follow his brother to the block, as his opponents on the Council grew stronger under Warwick's leadership. He was arrested and sent to the Tower, but was pardoned after having been made to confess to "negligence and incapacity." On this occasion he weathered the storm, but never again did he wield the same authority. His place, though not his title, was taken by Warwick, whom Mary knew she had more reason to fear than she had Somerset. In order to enlist aid for his cause, he had held out hopes of a Catholic revival and had tried to gain Mary's support. This she had denied him, with the Emperor's approval, though van der Delft had been sufficiently taken in by Warwick's promises to advise the contrary. How right Mary had been was proved by Warwick's *volte-face* when his coup was successful. He became even more demanding than his predecessor that the Protestant faith should be firmly established with no exceptions to the law.

Mary knew that she was again in great danger, and once more considered seriously the idea of leaving the country. The Emperor had previously suggested that marriage to the Catholic Don Luis of Portugal would provide a means of escape. This same scheme was revived. Van der Delft thought it might "suit the Lady very well" as she spent her days in great distress. Mary was "less desirous to marry than to find some other means of getting out of this realm."[9] The marriage plan was discussed at great length in 1549 and 1550, but without effect, as no agreement could be reached on the amount of Mary's dowry. The Emperor was lukewarm about Mary's wish to go and live at the court of his sister in the Netherlands. He did not know what to do with her if she left England, or who would support her. The English would obviously not help, and he did not want any extra call on his already strained financial resources. Charles continued, however, to affirm his support from afar, but the Council rightly doubted whether he was in a position to carry out any serious reprisals.

Edward wrote a stern letter to Mary asking her to obey him and accusing her of breaking his laws. Mary's attitude remained the same. She did not believe that he wrote his letters unaided. She begged him in return not to be influenced by one set of opinions alone, to wait until he was grown up to decide on religious matters. Elizabeth's attitude was completely different. She was reported as coming to court and being continually with the King. She was received "with great pomp and triumph." "It seems that they have a higher opinion of her for conforming with the others and observing the new decrees, than of the Lady Mary, who remains constant in the Catholic faith, and stays at her house twenty-eight miles from here without being either summoned or visited by the Council."[10]

The idea of escape appealed more and more to Mary. She implored the Emperor to arrange it for her. As a result a detailed plan was drawn up and ships were sent to wait for her off the English coast. But when it came to the point of actually leaving, Mary could not make up her mind whether to go or to stay. "I am like a little ignorant girl, and I care neither for my goods nor for the world, but only for God's service and my conscience."[11] At the same time she packed some of her property into "great long hopsacks, which would not look as though they contained anything heavy." As she had begged the Emperor to arrange her escape she was afraid to annoy him by not going. But she hated to leave her household who would be like "lost sheep" without her and might "even follow these new opinions." She reiterated that she would willingly stay were she able to live and serve God as she had done in the past.

In the end, her Controller of the Household, Rochester, decided for her. He believed that if she stayed quietly at home she would be left free to practice her religion privately. He had heard that Edward had not long to live (from soothsayers—but soothsayers were believed). If she was to succeed him, it was essential that she should be in the country when he died. Rochester also doubted whether she could get away safely. He was right. Watchers had been set on every church tower and at the end of every passage in case of an uprising in that part of the country. The Council was fully aware of everything that was happening and had taken steps to prevent Mary's escape. In July 1550 Edward VI recorded in his journal: "Sir John Gates sent into Essex to stop the going away of the Lady Mary."[12]

Mary had hesitated until van der Delft was driven to distraction. He was ill, and had asked in any case to be recalled at the time of her flight in case he was held responsible and put to death in England. He died a natural death shortly afterward, raving, it was said, about the whole arrangement. He had been replaced by Jehan Scheyve, another ambassador who had no very clear understanding of the religious and political situation in England—perhaps not surprisingly, since it changed so rapidly. He was, nevertheless, able to act as intermediary between the Emperor and Mary, as his predecessor had done, and was presumably also able to be of some comfort to the unfortunate Princess.

Mary had gained nothing by her attempt to escape. It was known or rumored all over Europe and served to strengthen Warwick's hand against her and the Emperor, though the Emperor and his sister firmly denied that there had ever been such a plot. Charles would willingly have shouldered the responsibility and would have added soothingly that Mary "had refused out of fear of offending her brother," but his sister had already gone too far in denials for that to be possible.

Warwick increased the pressure on Mary to conform. He had intelligence, which could only have come from someone inside Mary's household, that one of her priests had said Mass when she was not there. The priest was frightened and ran away, but was later caught and sent to prison. Mary was indignant. The Chancellor, Lord Rich, came to see her and expressed ignorance of any promise that had been made to allow her to practice the old religion.* Charles, when informed, said, "Our fears seem now to have been justified, for the very men who gave the promise, being still in the Council, appear to be inclined to disregard it."[13] But he saw the difficulty in proving a verbal promise given to a man who had since died. He therefore suggested to Mary that she might try to be a little more conciliatory and not go out of her way to provoke the Council. She should keep to her side of the bargain and only hear Mass in private—"not invite in the neighborhood," an accusation which he understood had been made against her. On March 18, 1551, Edward wrote in his journal that the Lady Mary had been summoned to Westminster to be told by his Council that he could no longer suffer her disobedience for " ... her example might breed too much inconvenience." Mary answered that her soul was God's, and that she would neither change her faith nor dissemble her opinion with contrary doings. This was a very terse summary of a spirited dialogue between Mary

*See page 93.

and the Council, in which she succeeded only in antago-
nizing Warwick by her provocative statements.

Two days later, the Emperor's ambassador
brought the message that his master would declare war
if his cousin could not " ... freely retain the ancient
religion in such sort as her father had left it in this realm,
according to a promise made to the Emperor, until the
King should be of more years."[14] The Council, following Rich's advice, denied that the King had made so
comprehensive a promise. They said that he had only
allowed " ... that she should for a season hear the Mass
in her closet or privy chamber only, whereat there
should be present no more than they of her chamber,
and no time appointed, but left to the King's pleasure."[15] When the Emperor heard this, he said, "Ought
it not suffice you that ye spill your own souls, but that ye
have a mind to force others to lose theirs too?"[16] The
Council's reply was to send at least two of Mary's servants to the Fleet Prison for having heard Mass.

In August, the Council informed the Emperor
that they were ready to compel Mary's obedience.
Three of Mary's household, including Rochester, were
then summoned before them and instructed to prevent
her four chaplains from saying Mass. They were given
letters to present to her. When they attempted to do so,
Mary was indignant that her own servants should be
called upon to tell her what she might and might not do.
She wrote immediately to her brother to tell him forci-
bly, though respectfully, how she viewed such interference. She repeated that she did not believe that he
acted of his own volition. "It is well known ... that
although our Lord be praised, your Majesty hath far
more knowledge, and greater gifts than others of your
years, yet it is not possible that your Highness can at
these years be a judge in matters of religion."[17] She
apologized for her "rude and bold letters" and politi-

cally signed herself, as usual, "Your Majesty's most humble sister."

Her servants returned to the Council bearing her letter with them. They reported their failure to obtain her ear and said how "marvellously offended" their mistress had been with them. "As she oftentimes altered her color, and seemed to be passioned and unquiet, they forbare to trouble her any further, fearing that the troubling of her might perchance bring her to her old disease."[18] When they were again instructed to go back to Mary and fulfil their commission, they refused, not finding it in their hearts or consciences to do so. They were sent to the Tower for their pains.

The Council sent a Commission under Lord Chancellor Rich with a replacement of their own persuasion for her loyal Controller, Rochester. Mary showed herself a true daughter of her mother in similar circumstances and argued stubbornly against them. She said that she would appoint her own officers, as she "had years sufficient for that purpose." "And," she added, "I am sickly, and yet I would not die willingly, but will do the best I can to preserve my life; but if I shall chance to die, I will protest openly that you of the Council be the cause of my death"[19]—surely a rhetorical threat. She could not in her heart believe that the Council would dare to use violence against her, and she knew that the legitimate punishment for disobedience was a fine or a short term in prison. She was prepared to let her servants go to prison, and they concurred in this, in order to satisfy the consciences of them all. She further asserted that if any of her servants were replaced by men of the Council's choice, she would leave the house at once.

The Commission could be said to have got the better of the argument only because they had the force of authority behind them. Mary's chaplains were co-

erced into agreeing not to allow Mass or any other service to be held except that provided for by the new laws
of the realm. They were to report any disobedience
immediately. Mary managed, however, to give the impression that she did not take her visitors very seriously.
As they were leaving, she called out to them from a
window with a message for them to take to the Council.
She asked that Rochester should soon be sent back to
her, "For," said she, "since his departing I take the account myself of my expenses, and learn how many
loaves of bread be made of a bushel of wheat, and ye wis
my father and my mother never brought me up with
baking and brewing, and to be plain with you, I am
weary of mine office."[20] Her request was not granted
and her servants did not come back to her until their
term of imprisonment had expired. But Mary realized
"that the orders were strict and precise," and so dismissed her chaplains. She remembered that the Emperor's sister had assured her (through Scheyve) that
God would never call her to account if, despite all argument, she had to put up with no Mass; the important
thing was that she should go on believing in the Mass.

To counter the argument that Mary might follow
her religion until the King came of age, Warwick (who
had created himself Duke of Northumberland) announced that the King was now indeed of age to make
his own decisions about the Lady Mary. Edward denied
that any promise had been made to her, and repeated
that she had only been allowed to hear Mass "subject to
his pleasure." His pleasure now was that she should
conform. She should have no privileges in regard to
hearing Mass in private but, he added, no force would
be applied to violate the Princess's conscience or to
make her adopt his religion. Thereafter, nothing more
is to be found in the record about Mary's religious struggle with the Council except for one letter she sent to the

Emperor. It is not easy to see why there was this change. Mary may have followed the Emperor's advice and have given no cause to the Council to molest her; she may have been more cautious in her observance of her religion; or she may have given up hearing Mass altogether in the belief that God would forgive her. This is borne out by the letter mentioned above which in March 1533 she sent to Charles as her "help and refuge," her "second spiritual father," to obtain that she could hear Mass in secret which for nearly two years past had been denied her.

Edward's health was also giving the Council cause for concern. Mary was next in line of succession. When she became Queen, she could be expected to remember and to punish anyone who had treated her badly. She had already shown that she possessed considerable strength of character, or obstinacy, depending on the point of view. It was known that she could count on support not only from the Emperor but from those nearer at hand, the English Catholics who had been suppressed but not converted. She was also a popular figure in the country as a whole, which could not be said about Northumberland.

The Protector had finally been overthrown by Northumberland in December 1551. He had again been sent to the Tower with many and varied charges against him. This time he was convicted (of felonious treason) and sentenced to death. On January 22 of the following year, Edward recorded in his journal: "The Duke of Somerset had his head cut off upon Tower Hill between eight and nine o'clock in the morning."[21] Edward had been persuaded by Northumberland to think his uncle an evil man and was seemingly undisturbed by his death, although he had petitioned the Council to spare his uncle's life. Northumberland's popularity was not enhanced by this method of ridding himself of a rival who had already been beaten, but he was afraid that their positions could be reversed and was taking no chances. He kept an even stricter watch over the King than before and regulated his visitors in order that no influence but his own could be brought to bear on him. Edward showed no signs of disagreement with his chief minister—and no signs of relenting toward Mary, except to leave her in peace.

Mary's servants returned to her in April. When not troubled by illness or fits of depression, she led what was for her an almost normal life. She studied; she sewed; she had the companionship of the Ladies and Gentlemen of her household; she visited and cared for the poor and the sick in her neighborhood. Her house was quiet and decorous. To some it might have appeared dull, but it was infinitely to be preferred to the discomforts, harassments and uncertainties of her former life. She was not cut off from the outside world and was free to entertain her friends, which she no doubt did with circumspection. But it would be unrealistic to think that holy thoughts and good deeds filled the whole of Mary's life. She could not have failed to hear the rumors of Edward's state of health and must have reflected a great deal as to what her actions should be when she became Queen. Certainly her cousin the Emperor had always had this possibility in mind. He would not otherwise have spent so much of his time and energy in her support.

In 1552, Edward had been afflicted with several illnesses which aggravated what is now considered to have been a tubercular condition. Mary came to visit him in June and was well received. In early February 1553, she made another of her rare visits. This time she was magnificently received at Westminster. Northumberland and other members of the Council went out of their way to do her honor as if to acknowledge that she was their future Queen. The King, however, was taken ill with a high fever the evening she arrived, and she was not allowed to see him for three days. Then she visited him in his bedchamber where "... the King received her very kindly and graciously and entertained her with small talk, making no mention of matters of religion."[22] Edward did not recover from this illness; he lingered on for another five months in a state of weakness not improved by the doctoring he received.

Northumberland was not only the most powerful man in the country; he was also the most unscrupulous. Edward's illness was a blow to him, for he foresaw that his own authority might end with the death of the King. The prospect that the Catholic Mary should become Queen in a comparatively short time filled him with dread for his future. He therefore evolved a plan intended to prevent her accession and at the same time increase his own stature and that of his family. His idea was to substitute Lady Jane Grey for Mary as heir to the throne and to marry one of his sons to Jane.

If Edward's days were numbered, as it now seemed, Northumberland had to move quickly. First, he arranged that Jane should marry his fourth son, Lord Guilford Dudley. After the death of Somerset, the last would-be arbiter of her fate, Jane had returned to her parents. Her father, the Marquis of Dorset, had been given his dead father-in-law's title of Duke of Suffolk and put on the Council by his friend Northumberland in 1551. He had nothing against the suggested arrangement, which in the circumstances seemed better than the one promoted by Thomas Seymour. The marriage took place in May 1553 when Jane was about fifteen years old.

By Act of Parliament Henry VIII had been given the right to name his successors. Edward was induced to override his father's will and to make his own will, secretly naming Lady Jane Grey as his heir. This will was signed on June 21 by Edward, the Privy Council and others. This time there was no publicized Act of Parliament to give him the authority. On the 23rd, the names of Mary and Elizabeth were omitted from the prayers in the churches.

Northumberland no doubt envisaged his grandson as a future King of England but, more immediately, himself as ruler to all intents and purposes, with his son and Jane Grey as puppets to be directed by him. Jane was not a party to this plan; nor, unhappy as her home life was, had she any wish to marry Guilford Dudley. She agreed because she had no alternative but to obey her parents. After her marriage, she went back home to her parents, and only occasionally visited her husband's family.

On Thursday, July 6, 1553, Edward VI died at Greenwich. Nine dramatic days, with tragic consequences, followed the death of the boy king.

# CHAPTER IV

# QUEEN JANE

Edward VI's death was kept generally secret for four days while Northumberland and the Council put the finishing touches to their plans. They were not fully prepared, for although they had known for some time that the King was dying, they did not know how long he would last. (There were indeed rumors that Northumberland had hastened his end.) The news of Edward's approaching death had spread to Europe, and the Pope, the King of France and the Emperor were waiting, ready to intervene if the opportunity presented itself. The Pope had to postpone any action to aid the re-establishment of the Catholic Church in England as he had no official representative there, but he had Cardinal Pole in mind as a candidate for the time when and if Mary became Queen. Antoine de Noailles, Henry II's new ambassador, had been appointed earlier in the year; Claude de l'Aubespine, Henry's Minister of State, had arrived in June; and two more of his envoys were on the French coast, waiting to be summoned. Once they had been given the word, the French were ready to send an army to aid Northumberland and the Council against the Emperor's cousin.

On June 23, the Emperor had sent three ambassadors—Jean de Courrières, Jacques de Thoulouse and Simon Renard—with his latest advice on how best to further Mary's cause at least cost to himself. By coincidence, they reached London on the Thursday Edward died. They were not informed officially, but heard the news the next day through their spies. More ominously, the Council did not tell Mary either. If she had continued her journey to London to see her brother as they hoped, she would have fallen into their hands. But some anonymous well-wisher who did not like to see justice overturned hastened the news to her. Not aware of the arrival of the Emperor's delegation, she quietly went away that same night, with only a few companions. Her intention was to reach Kenninghall in Norfolk, which had the double advantage of being further from London and nearer to friends. To justify her departure, she left word that she had had to return to Kenninghall because of an outbreak of illness among her servants.

Renard and his companions were somewhat taken aback to find that, without hearing what the Emperor had to say, she had decided to declare herself Queen as soon as she heard of the King's death. This was the custom in England, and it would also enable Mary to discover who were her friends and who were her enemies. She had everything to gain and nothing to lose. The ambassadors hurriedly sent a message after her to tell her of their arrival and to beg her not to undertake any such action without more careful consideration. She had however gone too far to be able to turn back, so she ignored their warning.

Thus Mary, who could never make up her own mind, went against the advice of the man she most

*Lady Jane Grey, married Lord Guildford
Dudley, son of the Duke of Northumberland. She was crowned Queen of England
(when 15 years old) and reigned for nine
days. She and her husband were beheaded,
February, 1554. (Attributed to Master
John.)*

trusted and set off on a course of her own. It was as though, when the moment arrived for her to become Queen, she was suddenly endowed with the qualities of decision and authority becoming a Queen. It is, however, more likely that her closest advisers, including the Earl of Sussex, Sir Robert Rochester, Sir Henry Jerningham, and Sir Henry Bedingfield, had already decided her tactics and she had accepted them. Mary never lacked the courage or stubbornness to carry out a line of conduct once it was established as the correct thing for her to do. Her religion had been settled for her from birth, so she never had any doubts about that. Perhaps also, as she had assumed from Henry VIII's will that she would succeed Edward, she believed that possession of the Crown was her right and that her proper course was to see that right acknowledged.

The Emperor and his ambassadors had the same end in view, but they would have gone about it more diplomatically and, as things turned out, certainly less successfully. The ambassadors did not think that Mary and her friends stood the slightest chance against the forces and the finances that Northumberland could command. "The actual possession of power was a matter of great importance, especially among barbarians like the English."[1] They were terrified that her actions would throw England into such confusion that the military presence of the Emperor would be necessary—and yet so difficult to provide. Mary, not possessing their diplomatic and political skill or knowledge of the unsatisfactory state of the Emperor's affairs, behaved the way she thought she should. She showed great determination, courage and initiative. Fortune too bestowed one of her rare smiles on Mary.

After hearing the news of Edward's death on July 6, Mary spent the same night in the house of a Catholic sympathizer at Sawston. Perhaps forewarned, she left early in the morning, but only just in time: Northumberland's men were close on her heels and set fire to the house thinking she was still in it. The next night, which passed without incident, she stayed at Hengrave Hall and on the ninth she reached her home at Kenninghall. From here she sent out proclamations of her accession and started to raise an army. She also wrote to the Council expressing her surprise that they had not come to do her homage and requesting them to proclaim her in London.

The Imperial ambassadors in London were in a dilemma. They could not now act as intermediaries between Mary and the Emperor. They could get no appointment with Northumberland (which was not surprising in the circumstances), and were therefore unable to communicate to him the Emperor's messages of good will and reassurance as to his intentions in regard to Mary. Nor were they able to implant a few seeds of suspicion as to the intentions of the French in regard to England. Their instructions were out of date, and the Emperor was too far away to keep up with events. On July 10, the Council sent Sir William Petre and Sir William Cecil to inform them officially of the King's death. The ambassadors were apparently not told then, but gathered from their own efficient sources of information, that Guilford Dudley and Jane Grey were to be crowned King and Queen later that same day, according to Northumberland's plan.

During this time Northumberland had not been idle. He sent one of his sons at the head of another troop of soldiers to bring in Mary while he directed affairs from London or from his house up the river at Sion. The Mayor and Aldermen of the City of London and the Guards of Greenwich Palace and the Tower were the first to be told of Edward's death and of the contents of his will. Astonished they may have been, but they dutifully swore allegiance to the new Queen. On Sunday, the same day that Mary reached Kenninghall, Jane Grey, who was with her parents, was summoned urgently to join her husband at Sion House, where she heard for the first time that Edward was dead. Although she may already have been told that he had named her as his successor, she was still immensely shocked at the news and collapsed into tears. Her first reaction was to refuse, but the joint persuasion of her parents, her husband, Northumberland and the four members of the Council who were present eventually wore down her resistance. She prayed for divine guidance but heaven gave no sign, so she decided reluctantly to obey the dictates of her elders and the wishes of the late King.

The next day, July 10, Jane and Guilford Dudley came in state down the Thames to the Tower where, at five o'clock in the evening, Jane was proclaimed Queen with a fitting ceremony. But she absolutely refused to consider the idea that Guilford should become King, much to the surprise and anger both of her husband and his parents. If Jane had been pushed into the position she now held, she was going to exercise the prerogative of that position. It seems amazing today to think that a fifteen-year-old girl with no experience beyond a studious, unhappy home life should have had the courage to stand up to Northumberland, a man whose authority and compelling presence were such that all the members of the Council were subservient to him. Perhaps, as with Mary, it was ignorance of the possible consequences that enabled Jane to speak her mind so freely.

The Heralds then went out into London to broadcast the news that Jane was Queen, and that the Ladies Mary and Elizabeth were illegitimate. (The death of Edward had been announced earlier in the day.) The people were as unenthusiastic as Jane herself. Perhaps

they were just stunned, as they had expected Mary to be
Queen. Although Mary had led a retired life, she was
popular. Her goodness and virtue were proverbial, and
she had the esteem, the pity and the affection of the
country as a whole.

The ambassadors still thought Mary had embarked
on an extremely dangerous enterprise and did not consider that the great love the English people bore her was
enough to ensure her success. The Emperor agreed with
them: "Not much trust may be placed in the devotion
and affection certain private individuals and the people
profess for her; for unless a number of the most powerful nobles took her side it would be impossible to coun-
termine the carefully prepared course of action that
Northumberland is working out with, as you suspect,
the help of France."[2]

The ambassadors feared for her life but were
powerless to help, even with words, as they were forbidden to communicate with her. This was perhaps a good
thing, as it happened, for their words would certainly
have tended to discourage her. They also feared for
their own safety, as they had been informed that their
mission was over and that there was nothing to keep
them in England any longer. (De Noailles had used his
not inconsiderable influence with the Council to help
achieve this end.) Renard and his companions made
preparations to leave, but they doubted whether they
would be able to cross the Channel which they had
heard was heavily guarded by English ships to prevent
any attempt at escape by Mary. They put as cogently as
possible what they imagined to be the Emperor's point
of view, stressing his friendly attitude to the Duke and
the Council, the success he was having in his wars in
Europe and urging the Council to protect and shelter
the Lady Mary. Their conciliatory tactics brought them

*Henry Grey, Duke of Suffolk, father of Jane Grey. Twelve days after death of his daughter, he was also beheaded in February, 1554. (From the original by Mark Gerard.)* THE TRUSTEES OF THE BRITISH MUSEUM.

respite and, before they were ready to leave, the situation had completely changed and it was no longer necessary for them to do so.

Jane and the Council stayed on in the Tower as a security measure until the real temper of the country could be judged. On Tuesday the eleventh, Mary's letter from Kenninghall arrived and created consternation. The Duchess of Northumberland cried and so did the Duchess of Suffolk—but presumably tears of mortification and anger, not of regret for having betrayed an old friend through ambition. Not only was Mary still at liberty, but she had had the effrontery to demand their allegiance. The Council dissembled their feeling of unease. They wrote back to tell her that her illegitimacy precluded any right she might mistakenly think she had to the throne and that she should recognize the legitimate Queen appointed by Edward VI to succeed him. They decided also to send a strong force of men to rout her local supporters and to bring her back a prisoner. The Duke of Suffolk was chosen to lead them. This time it was Jane who cried. She begged her father to stay with her. He was at any rate the devil she knew. Northumberland reluctantly agreed to go in his place, though he rightly feared that in his absence the Council might not present a united front.

When Mary heard that Jane had been proclaimed Queen and that Northumberland was on his way, she withdrew to Framlingham in Suffolk, a castle which had formerly belonged to the Duke of Norfolk. More and more people flocked to her side from the surrounding counties and from further afield in response to her call for supporting troops.* But even so, when Mary received the letter from the Council her courage failed her. She appealed to the ambassadors to enlist the Emperor's support, for she saw "destruction hanging over her" unless she received his help. They dared not reply.

If ever there was a time of uncertainty it was now. The Emperor was several days behind in hearing the latest news, and it was several days later still before his ambassadors received his instructions. The ambassadors were not fully informed of the state of affairs in England, and were hampered moreover by the fact that they spoke no English. The Council did not know what action the Emperor might undertake on Mary's behalf, while Mary could not gauge the strength of the opposition she had to face. And Northumberland, once he had

*It is not known how many. The numbers estimated varied from hundreds to tens of thousands.

left London, could sense the disaffection among the Council and his soldiers.

All these facts played into Mary's hands and, as the Emperor was later to say, she was saved by a miracle. The English fleet waiting in the Channel was driven ashore by storms, and the sailors were won over by Jerningham who met them by chance when he went to reconnoiter. He was said to have brought back a hundred guns and a thousand men to reinforce Mary's defenses. Money, ammunition and provisions continued to pour in. City after city declared for Mary until soon it was clear the whole country was behind her.

Northumberland had set out on the fourteenth, presumably full of hope, though he commented on the apathy of the citizens who watched him leave London. Nobody wished him well. His last task had been to exhort the Council to loyalty and to urge the ministers of religion to do all in their power to support Jane's cause and denigrate Mary. Nicholas Ridley, Bishop of London, carried out his orders with zeal when he preached on the following Sunday, the sixteenth, unaware that by then Northumberland had failed. When he realized his faux pas, Ridley hurried to Mary, hoping to make amends, but his effort was in vain and he was sent to the Tower. Even the Emperor's ambassadors were cheered by the news that filtered through to London and began to think that perhaps after all Mary stood a chance.

As Northumberland had feared, Suffolk lacked the necessary authority to hold together the Council. Morale was low and the Council freely discussed whether they should come out in force for Mary or stay with Jane. With their own futures in view, they opted for what they thought would be the winning side. Gradually they moved out of the Tower to Baynard's Castle a short distance up the river (only Suffolk stayed behind with his daughter), where the Earl of Arundel addressed them in no uncertain terms: "If we look at my Lady Mary we shall see her endowed with all the best gifts, so that we may only expect real justice, perpetual peace, lasting mercifulness, unbounded clemency and excellent government."[3] And he reminded his listeners of the dangers of civil war and possible invading armies from both France and the Empire. (There had been talk that Northumberland was negotiating the exchange of the remaining English possessions in France in return for French military support against Mary.) The Earl of Pembroke supported Arundel. On the eighteenth, the Council switched their allegiance from Jane to Mary and offered a reward for Northumberland's arrest.

Suffolk was summoned from the Tower in order to get his assent to the new proclamation. He signed without demur, then went back to tell his daughter before he too abandoned her. Jane was not unwilling to give up the crown. She said she knew it rightly belonged to Mary, and the part she herself had played had been prepared for her without her knowledge. She and her husband stayed on in the Tower, deserted by all those who had brought them there, including Jane's attendants.

On the nineteenth, a delegation from the Council informed the Imperial ambassadors of the new state of affairs. They were amazed and at first suspected trickery—"they almost thought they might be dreaming." But at four o'clock in the afternoon Mary was indeed proclaimed Queen at Paul's Cross. And this time the crowds rejoiced. Bells were rung, there were bonfires in the streets, and the Council went to St. Paul's to hear the *Te Deum*, which had not been sung there for some years. Arundel and Paget went off to lay the submission of the Council at Mary's feet. And so ended the nine days of the reign of Queen Jane.

*Mary, age 38. Crowned Queen of England, July 19, 1553. (Antonio Moro) ISABELLA GARDNER MUSEUM. BOSTON.*

# CHAPTER V

# MARY THE QUEEN

## 1. First Days

Mary's surprise at the dramatic turn of events without need for any military confrontation must have been as great as Northumberland's, and certainly more pleasurable. She left Framlingham for London and on the way stopped at New Hall, where she met for the first time Simon Renard and his companions. They were very punctilious in their behavior on this and later occasions, trying not to give the impression that they had any Imperial secrets and advice to impart in private. De Noailles too rode out to pay his homage, more because that was the correct thing to do than to make amends for the French intrigues against her in the past or with any intention of changing his behavior in the future. Elizabeth, who had remained quietly in Hatfield all this month of July waiting to see the outcome, had neither responded to Northumberland's request for support nor offered friendly aid to Mary. She now wrote a letter of congratulations, asking at the same time whether, when she came to salute her, she should wear robes of celebration or of mourning. (If her intention was to be snide in reminding her sister that, in all upheaval, the late King was still unburied and unmourned in his coffin at Westminster, it was unnecessary: Mary was very much troubled whether her brother's last rites should be according to the religion which he had followed for most of his lifetime or the one in which she herself wholeheartedly believed.)

Mary made her first state entrance into London on August 3, dressed in a robe of violet velvet with the "skirt and sleeves embroidered with gold." She was accompanied by a large number of the nobility and escorted by about a thousand* soldiers on horseback and on foot. A large part of her army had already been disbanded on the way to London. Behind her rode Elizabeth with her retinue, all of whom had been affectionately greeted by Mary. The procession made its way through the rejoicing multitudes to the Tower, where Mary took up residence in the State Apartments lately vacated by Jane. She was so closely guarded that the Emperor's ambassadors were not able to speak to her. It was too soon to be absolutely sure that she had no treachery to fear from the former insurgents.

Mary waited in the Tower until Edward VI's funeral had taken place on August 8. Edward was buried in the Henry VII chapel in Westminster Abbey, with a Protestant service conducted by Thomas Cranmer, Archbishop of Canterbury. Mary's conscience was troubled at this decision, but the ambassadors had persuaded her of the folly of introducing drastic changes too quickly. "It has also occurred to us," they said, "that the ceremonies observed at funerals touch religion less nearly than others, and are therefore less objectionable to conscience."[1] She compromised, with the agreement of the Council, by attending herself a Catholic service,

---

*Another report says five thousand.

conducted by Stephen Gardiner, Bishop of Winchester, in the church in the Tower. Three hundred members of the nobility accompanied her, but Elizabeth was not among them. Mary then went to Richmond until the middle of September when she came back to London to arrange for her coronation.

One of Mary's first acts on entering the Tower had been to free the old Duke of Norfolk, who had been there since the last days of Henry VIII, the Bishops Gardiner and Tunstal, Lady Somerset (the Lord Protector's widow) and Edward Courtenay, whose mother was one of Mary's greatest friends. Courtenay had been a prisoner since his father's execution in 1538 and was now about twenty-six years old. Mary showed her favor by bestowing on him his father's titles of Marquis of Exeter and Earl of Devon. The rumor was current that he was a possible husband for the new Queen, and many people would have favored such a marriage.

Northumberland had been declared a rebel and brought back to the Tower to await trial. The Council all tried to save themselves and denied that they had acted of their own free will, in spite of evidence to the contrary: their signatures were at the bottom of Edward VI's will and Jane's proclamation. Mary " ... could not help being amazed by the divisions in the Council ... (so) that she was unable to get at the truth of what had happened with regard to the will of the King, her brother, or the plots that had been woven to her hurt."[2] But, as she preferred to be "liked for her mercifulness than hated for her justice," she was lenient. Of twenty-seven people named as rebels, most were pardoned. Only three were executed: the Duke of Northumberland and two of his principal supporters, Sir John Gates and Sir Thomas Palmer. Some, including Jane and her husband, were kept in the Tower as a safety measure, but Jane's father and mother were allowed to go free. Mary would have spared them all. "It is greatly to be feared that the impunity bestowed by her clemency may turn to her own hurt and give occasion for evil-doing. Indeed, it seems to be necessary rather to encourage her to have justice done than to temper the rigor of punishment,"[3] wrote the ambassadors to the Emperor, in reply to his advice that she should not be too severe in her reprisals. The Emperor, however, believed that the chief insurgents, including Jane, should be dealt with severely, but only got his way as far as Northumberland and his two friends were concerned.

Northumberland met his death, so it was said, on the same scaffold erected for his father, Edmund Dudley, forty-five years earlier to the day. In the end he proved not to have the courage of his avowed convictions. He pleaded guilty at this trial (though not to having poisoned Edward VI) and gave up his Protestant beliefs, affirming that he had without any compulsion re-embraced the Catholic faith. Gates and Palmer followed his example. Jane, in the Tower at the time of his execution, was reported to have been shocked that Northumberland should have tried to obtain pardon by his conversion. It was natural that she should express her indignation that he had brought her and her family into "the most miserable calamity and misery by his extreme ambition." Even in so young a girl, however, her religious conviction was stronger than her desire to live. "Should I, who (am) young," she said, "forsake my faith for the love of life?"[4] And these were not empty words, as she was later to prove. She was as ardent a Protestant as Mary was a Catholic.

Now that Mary was Queen the Emperor hoped to use his influence over her to his own advantage. He wanted to be assured of a continually friendly England to support him in his struggles against both the French and the dissidents in his own dominions. He realized that he must act discreetly so as not to alienate the English people or incite the French to further intrigues.

Four ambassadors were too conspicuous, and in any case excessive. After less than three months, he recalled three of them, leaving only Renard as his capable (though underpaid) representative at Mary's Court. Renard, however, had to postpone the pleasure of being left in sole charge of Mary, for she, partly in her generosity of spirit and partly to show her gratitude, invited the others to stay on until after her Coronation—an invitation which they had no hesitation in accepting. The Emperor bombarded Mary, either directly or more often through his envoys, with lengthy advice which she humbly acknowledged. He exaggerated the lengths to which he had gone in order to help her gain the throne, with a view to making her feel beholden to him. For example, he had talked of sending armed vessels to English waters under pretence of guarding his herring fleet fishing off the coast, but it is doubtful whether he had time to send them before the victory had gone to Mary. But we find Mary submissively appreciative of his kindness "in equipping men-of-war to come to my assistance."

Mary had no knowledge of worldly matters or affairs of state as Renard had discovered: "I know the Queen to be good, easily influenced, inexpert in worldly matters and a novice all round; and the English so grasping that if one cares to try them with presents and promises one may do what one likes with them by very simple means ... I believe that if God does not preserve her she will be deceived and lost either by the machinations of the French, the conspiracies of the English, by poison or otherwise."[5] Mary had lived most of her life away from the seat of power and had not been trained for her present position. Machiavelli had not been on her reading list. She admitted that she had so much business she did not know where to begin. For support she had to rely on many people whose loyalty she did not trust. Once she had put her few reliable friends in office she had to fill up the rest of the posts from the old Council, who were at any rate experienced in the art of governing even if not trustworthy. But in so doing she alienated some of the nobles who had expected to be rewarded for coming to her aid. Mary's natural kindliness generally led her in the right direction. She did her best to care for the poor, the sick, the hungry and the afflicted—who had greatly increased in number and were more in need of assistance since the closure of the monasteries, their former source of succor. She promised to pay off the debts left by her father and brother and she remitted the most burdensome of the taxes that had been imposed in Edward's reign. But she herself was poor and had no private means with which to reward her own friends and faithful retainers, and her conscience would not let her make use of any revenue still to be obtained from the sale of Church lands. It was for Gardiner, in his new post as Chancellor, to raise funds which could be placed at her disposal, a task for which he was well qualified. Mary herself however did not give up her love of fine clothes, and the court, which had been somberly clad since the death of Henry VIII, again blossomed forth in silks and velvets of brilliant hue.

The Emperor, who by contrast with Mary was world-weary and overexperienced in dealing with wily opponents on both political and religious fronts, urged Mary to be prudent and to beware of excessive zeal: not to make any changes in religion or introduce unpopular policies until she could do so with the approval of Parliament. She had first to show herself a good Englishwoman bent wholly on her country's good. His advice was sound—and necessary. Left to her own devices, and prompted by Gardiner, Mary would have started reforms immediately. But she listened to the Emperor

*The Emperor Charles V., father of Philip II. (Lucas Cranach) Thyssen-Bornemisza Collection, Lugano)*

and, apart from the reintroduction of Mass into the church services, was slow to make any official move.

Mary's own immediate circle was made up entirely of Catholics and she rarely mixed with people who admitted to being Protestants. She had no idea how much England had changed in the twenty years since her father had denied the Pope. The young people in particular—the contemporaries of Elizabeth and Jane Grey, who had never been subjected to the Roman church—tended to follow the new forms of religion. Though Mary still had a Catholic following among older people and throughout the country as a whole, London itself was mostly Protestant. The citizens reacted against even her minor innovations. There were murmurings against Edward VI's funeral service in the Tower, and near riots in a city church where Mass was reinstated and at Paul's Cross, where an inflammatory sermon was preached. The disturbances caused Mary, on August 18, to issue her first royal proclamation on a religious issue—a modest one, but with undertones of sterner measures to come. First, she stated categorically that she herself would continue to follow the Catholic faith which she had practiced since birth. She hoped that all her subjects would do the same of their own free will; she did not desire to compel any one to do so *for the present* (author's italics). But until new ordinances were made, all should try to live together in Christian charity, eschewing such words as *papist, heretic* and so forth.

The mild tone of this proclamation shows that Mary was trying to be prudent and cautious. But what is very interesting to note is the reference she goes on to make to the dangers of representations (plays), illicitly printed books, rhymes and ballads. In less than eighty years the printed word had become in England the powerful vehicle of propaganda which before the days of Caxton could only have been spread slowly by word of mouth and through copies made by scriveners. It was a forcible weapon in the hands of the rebellious. Appreciation of this fact led Mary to continue: "Neither shall they print any book, treatise, dialogue, rhyme, ballad, comedy or argument except by special written command of her Majesty, under pain of her displeasure."[6]

Mary's instructions were not obeyed in London. Argument and dissension continued. A rumor that Cranmer had said Mass in Canterbuy Cathedral moved him to write a *Declaration* stating in no uncertain terms his support of the Church of Edward VI. For this he was sent to the Tower to join Nicholas Ridley, Bishop of London. Behind Cranmer lay a whole series of heinous crimes, in Mary's eyes. It was he who had declared null the marriage between Henry VIII and Katharine of Aragon. The fact that he had done the same for Henry's marriage to Anne Boleyn did not mitigate his offenses. During the reign of Edward VI he had brought together the Church of England and Protestant reformers in Europe. He was responsible for the first prayer book. He had twice made himself liable to a charge of high treason: the first time by signing Edward VI's will instigated by Northumberland; the second, by signing the Proclamation of Jane. Hugh Latimer, Bishop of Worcester, followed Cranmer into the Tower. They could both have avoided imprisonment, as so many of their fellow churchmen did, by escaping to cities abroad where their doctrines would have been acceptable. The Council gave them every opportunity to leave, but they chose to stay. The exodus of the Protestant churchmen was accompanied by the flight of many foreigners who had come from Catholic Europe to England at the time when England was a Protestant haven. Some saw the writing on the wall and went of their own free will; others were asked to leave.

Mary had to steer her way through uncharted reefs and took the Emperor for her guiding star. She did not know that in his mind, her progress and the re-

*Edward Courtenay. Made Marquis of Exeter and Earl of Devon by Mary on her succession. Favored by some as husband for Mary. Died in exile in Padua, 1556. (Artist unknown, engraved by J. Cochran.)* **TRUSTEES OF THE BRITISH MUSEUM.**

establishment of the Catholic Church were secondary to the welfare of his Empire. Her Council were not trustworthy and disagreed among themselves. "She has more regard for Pole than all her Council put together,"[7] said Renard. The French, in the person of the intriguer de Noailles, were to be considered a danger at all times. Elizabeth, now twenty years old, was ambitious and ready to listen to the dissident voices of those willing to have her as their figurehead. Even Mary's friends were not necessarily qualified pilots. Gardiner had much in his past to make him suspect: he too had worked for the divorce of Mary's parents and had supported Henry VIII in his breakaway from the Pope. His nature was not an easy one: his temper was short and he was tactless and rough in manner, easily alienating friend and opponent alike. When his mind was made up he could be as stubborn as his Queen. His wish to press on with religious reform was dangerous however, for the Protestants, though temporarily quiet, formed too large a proportion of the country to be repressed without the risk of rebellion.

It was de Noailles' task to undermine the influence of the Emperor. Although France was a Catholic country, it was to her interest to bring down Mary and therefore to support the Protestants. It was worth her while making friendly overtures to anyone who could become a rallying point for dissension. Elizabeth and Edward Courtenay were obvious targets. Courtenay himself had high aspirations. The suggestion that he should marry the Queen did not displease him, but if he could not marry the Queen he could marry Elizabeth with the intention of ousting the Queen. The French encouraged this liaison. It was not so much that they preferred Elizabeth to Mary, but any means to get rid of Mary was acceptable to them. And afterward, if it was not Elizabeth they chose to support but Mary, Queen of

Scots who was betrothed to their own Dauphin, there was little redress Elizabeth could claim.

The Emperor's ambassadors reported the collusion between Courtenay, Elizabeth and de Noailles, hoping to needle Mary into doing something to restrain them. Elizabeth's attitude to religion was also disturbing. She professed herself a Protestant because she had been brought up in that faith. Mary subjected her to her own example of intensive prayer and hearing Mass several times a day, hoping to convince her of the error of her ways. Elizabeth apparently capitulated and was converted to Catholicism, but she still did not attend Mass. Nobody believed she had really been converted. Renard said she was "clever and sly" and should be watched lest "out of ambition or being persuaded thereto (she might) conceive some dangerous design and put it into execution."[8] Mary said the same consideration had already occurred to her and she already had it in mind to send Elizabeth away. She made no immediate move, but it was clear that her attitude to her younger sister had changed. She was no longer protective but highly suspicious.

The Emperor had no illusions about Mary's competence as Queen, nor indeed any high opinion of the capability of women in general. He did not attribute to her the qualities which had distinguished their grandmother, Isabella of Spain—though he might also have been hesitant about Isabella's success without the assistance of Ferdinand. By taking the government of Spain into his own hands, he had shown total disregard for his own mother, who was probably less mad than the world was led to believe. It is true that he had allowed his wife to be the titular head in Spain when he was away and his sister to rule the Netherlands; but they had remained under his guidance, as he hoped Mary would. Renard reported him as believing that a "great part of the labor of government could with difficulty be undertaken by a woman, and was not within woman's province, and also that it was important that the Queen should be assisted, protected and comforted in the discharge of those duties."[9] This was leading up to the suggestion that Mary should, therefore, give up her often declared desire for chastity and take herself a husband. In fact, however, the Emperor already had a husband in mind for her—his own son Philip.

Renard had no difficulty in gradually convincing Mary that Philip, in spite of his youth, was the man she should marry. As it turned out, this was the worst advice she could have followed. As a private individual, Mary would never have considered marriage for herself. As Queen, she agreed that it would be for the good of the realm for her to take a husband. She was given conflicting advice, but from the beginning put herself into the Emperor's hands. All that she asked of him was that, when arranging a suitable match for her, he should bear in mind that she was thirty-seven years of age.

Stephen Gardiner pressed her to marry Edward Courtenay, whom he had known in the Tower. But Courtenay, handsome, young and dashing, had found freedom intoxicating. His reputed way of life was not one that would appeal to Mary's strait-laced tastes. Still searching for an Englishman, Gardiner then thought of Reginald Pole, whose name had been linked with hers in the past. But Pole did not wish for marriage. He was already wedded to the Roman church. He also did not advise marriage for Mary, believing that in view of her age and the unlikelihood of her bearing children, she should remain single and let Henry VIII's wishes in regard to the succession take effect. The Council considered four foreign princes, none of whom would have pleased the Emperor any more than Courtenay or Pole had done. They would have pleased the English people even less. But before Mary could make any move in regard to religion or marriage, she had first to be crowned and a new Parliament had to be convened. Therefore though the problems were discussed, nothing was decided.

## 2. *Coronation and First Parliament*

In September Mary moved from Richmond to St. James's Palace, and then to the Tower, where it had long been customary for the Sovereign to reside immediately before the Coronation. Here she unexpectedly summoned the Council to her presence. Sinking to her knees in front of them, she addressed them at length in such a fashion that when she had finished there was not a dry eye among them. She spoke particularly of the duties of Kings and Queens and how she hoped with their help to carry out the task God had given her. Some ascribed the unusual humility of the speech to timidity on her part, but all were touched by her evident goodness and integrity.

Two days later, on September 30, 1553, at two o'clock in the afternoon, Mary and the procession left the Tower. They passed by way of Fenchurch, Gracechurch, Cornhill, Cheapside, St. Paul's Churchyard, Ludgate and Fleet Street to Whitehall Palace. All the way they were protected by the Queen's Guard. Various houses suspected of hiding weapons to be used against her had been searched. But in spite of all fears, everything passed off smoothly. The crowds were peaceful. The streets were decorated with flowers, tapestries and triumphal arches. The conduits in the City flowed with wine instead of water.

Elaborate pageants had been arranged at strategic points by various organizations, both foreign and English. The Florentines had a cleverly contrived setting for their pageant on the top of which, very high "stood an angel all in green, with a trumpet in his hand, and when the trumpeter who stood secretly in the pageant, did sound his trump, the angel did put his trumpet to his mouth, as though it had been the same that had sounded, to the great marvelling of many ignorant persons"[10]—and to the amusement of the rest, no doubt.

On behalf of the Mayor and the City Mary was presented with a purse containing a thousand pieces of gold. In St. Paul's Churchyard, John Heywood, the playwright who had on several occasions entertained Mary with his company of child actors, made an oration to her in Latin and English. "Peter a Dutchman stood on the weathercock of Paul's steeple, holding a streamer in his hand of five yards long, and waving thereof, stood some time on the one foot, and shook the other, and then kneeled on his knees, to the great marvel of all people."[11] The choristers of St. Paul's sang to the accompaniment of their viols. Ludgate had been repaired, newly painted and hung with tapestries, with minstrels playing and singing there. And as the procession passed along Fleet Street, it was seen that the old Temple Bar had also been newly painted and hung with tapestries.

Clad in a robe of purple velvet furred with powdered ermine, and wearing a small crown of precious stones which was so heavy that she had to support her head in her hand, Mary was carried in a chariot covered with gold tissue drawn by six horses trapped with the same. Before her, five hundred nobles, gentlemen and ambassadors rode on horseback followed by the Council, thirteen new Knights of the Bath,* the

*It was customary for the Sovereign to bathe in the nude with the newly created Knights of the Bath, but Mary had delegated this duty to the Earl of Arundel.

Lord Chancellor, the Lord High Treasurer, the Duke of Norfolk, the Earl of Oxford and the Mayor of London, in a gown of crimson velvet, carrying the scepter of gold. Behind her, in a chariot covered with cloth of silver drawn by four horses covered with like material were Elizabeth and Anne of Cleves dressed in robes of silver. There followed two other chariots covered in red satin (the occupants are not mentioned by name) and gentlewomen, some in gowns of red velvet riding on horses clad in red velvet, some in red satin and others in crimson satin. When eventually, after many stops, the procession reached Whitehall Palace, the Queen said farewell to the Mayor and thanked him and the City of London for all the trouble they had taken.

The next day Mary and her companions travelled the very short distance from Whitehall to the palace of Westminster by boat, and then went on foot over a blue-carpeted walk to Westminster Abbey. In a long elaborate ceremony lasting from ten in the morning until five in the afternoon, Mary was crowned Queen of England according to the *just and licit laws* of the realm—a clause introduced by Mary to cover herself in case she unwittingly accepted any part of the Protestant reforms during the course of the service. (She had even been suspicious of the anointing oils procurable in England, and had sent to the Bishop of Arras for the genuine Catholic product.) Mary had studied the oath she was to take and wished it to be according to the "old practice." She had also said that she did not wish to take the title of Head of the Church—although she had allowed herself to be proclaimed with this title in July before she knew that she had in fact been recognized as Queen. But in these matters she had to tread carefully, as Parliament had not as yet had the opportunity to make any decisions on religious or any other matters.

Stephen Gardiner, Bishop of Winchester, officiated at the ceremony, assisted by seven other bishops and clergymen. Mary first wore a robe of silver brocade covered with a cape of crimson velvet but she changed her attire three times during the day. She replaced her robes of state with a simple dress of purple velvet. Later, she appeared in white taffeta to receive the investments and regalia and to be crowned with the three crowns of England, Ireland and France (for England still held on to Calais and a small portion of the French coast much begrudged them by the French). After Mass she again retired to her private room in the Abbey, and this time came out clad in a black velvet cloak with a collar of ermine and lined with ermine. She carried in her right hand the royal scepter and in her left the royal sphere.

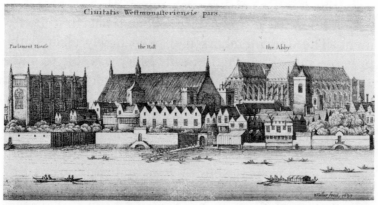

*Westminster, showing Parliament, the Great Hall and the Abbey, where Mary was crowned on October 1, 1553 and buried on December 14, 1558. (From an engraving by Mollar, 1647.) FOLGER SHAKESPEARE LIBRARY, WASHINGTON, D.C.*

Behind her stood Elizabeth and Anne of Cleves in robes of crimson velvet lined with ermine and on their heads crowns of gold ablaze with precious stones. Other ladies were dressed in scarlet. Renard faithfully recorded the whole procedure whereby Mary was crowned with a pomp and ceremony, he said, far grander in England than anywhere else. He described how the proclamation was read to the congregation who were then asked if they would accept Mary as their Queen—to which they all answered yes. He also noted that Elizabeth and the French ambassador exchanged glances of significance. Afterward, there was a big banquet in Westminster Hall where Mary sat on the stone of Scone once used by the Kings of Scotland when they were crowned. "She rested her feet on two of her ladies, which is also part of the prescribed ceremonial at such times."[12]

Four days later Mary opened her first Parliament. The 430 members had been newly elected the previous month, so theoretically Mary was able to make a fresh start. But even though newly elected, many of the members of both houses had also served under Northumberland and were not necessarily Catholic in outlook. They immediately received an inkling of what lay ahead. Mary could not separate religion from politics. So, clad in her robes of state and accompanied by all the Lords, spiritual and temporal, the Queen first attended Mass sung in St. Margaret's Church before proceeding to Westminster. The Chancellor welcomed her with a speech praising the virtues of their newly crowned Queen, which was well received both by the Lords and the Commons. Then Parliament got down to business and worked until they rose again in December.

The acts they passed were moderate ones. They were engaged in an attempt to put back the clock, but the question was how far back they should go. In the end, they settled for the last year of the reign of Henry

VIII. Mary was disappointed. She had hoped to restore the papal authority, but Parliament was not yet ready to go so far or to take any steps toward the restitution of church property. The specter of the Pope was a real one in England. Nevertheless, Parliament started off on the right path from Mary's point of view. Her first priority was that her own legitimacy and legitimate right to the throne should be confirmed by the recognition of her parents' marriage as just and lawful. By repealing the Act whereby the marriage had been annulled, Parliament was able to avoid any need to refer to the Pope or to the edict in which he had belatedly acknowledged the validity of the original dispensation permitting her parents to marry.* Even if Parliament had wished to use this document it would not have been easy to produce a copy. The affirmation of Mary's legitimacy was some solace to her after twenty-one years of disgrace, but was hardly likely to please Elizabeth, whose illegitimacy was automatically reaffirmed, as she had been born to Anne Boleyn during the lifetime of Katharine of Aragon.

Mary's first Parliament also repealed the religious laws passed during the reign of Edward VI. Cranmer's prayer book was replaced (though it was to be brought back again in the reign of Elizabeth) by the old service used in the reign of Henry VIII. The clergy were again forbidden to marry. The laws relating to treason and felony (which had been changed during the reign of Henry in an attempt to compel the subservience of those opposed to the divorce, and during the reign of Edward as a means of controlling the Catholics) were changed back into their earlier form. The *Statute of Uniformity*, which had caused so much distress to Mary, was repealed. Certain families or individuals who had been in disgrace were restored to favor, such as the

*See page 38.

Poles and the Exeters. Others were accused of high treason, including Cranmer and Lady Jane Grey and her husband, but no action was taken against them at this time.

Even though the measures were moderate by Mary's standards, they were strong enough to incite the more violent Protestants to action. Renard reported to the Emperor: "On the day Parliament rose, a dog with a shaven crown, clipped ears and a rope round his neck was thrown into the presence chamber with a scandalous writing attached to it, signifying that the priests and bishops should be hanged. The Queen was displeased at this, and told Parliament that such acts might move her to a kind of justice further removed from clemency than she could wish."[13] Mary's feeling was reinforced by a fanatical memoir sent her by Reginald Pole, who had been too long away from England to know what the real situation was. "Her Majesty must not allow herself to be intimidated by the counsellors possessed of little prudence and haply insincere, who may aver that dealing with questions of religion will bring about danger of tumults.... Let not her Majesty be satisfied with saying: 'My religion is sincere and spotless as it ever was....' Now that the kingdom is entrusted to her care, it is not enough that she should honor God; she must compel her subjects to do likewise, and punish the disobedient in virtue of the authority she has received from God.... She must use force to bring about what reason may fail to accomplish. Promptitude is necessary, and no time must be given for evil tendencies to gain in strength."[14] When to exhortations such as this was added Pole's advice to Mary against marriage, it is not surprising that the Emperor, who had been urging sweet reasonableness and a gradual approach to change, wished to delay the arrival in England of this fiery Cardinal.

## 3. *Marriage Plans*

The other great problem apart from religion, yet inextricably tied up with it, was the question of Mary's marriage. Various candidates had been proposed. Mary would have left it to the Emperor to decide, trusting that he would do what was best for her and for her country. He appreciated however that the choice had to appear to have been made by Mary, but that she had actually to be led to make the choice herself. As the English hated foreigners, the Emperor could not take any action which might lead them to believe that he was interfering. This was the kind of ingenious operation which must have appealed to him. He was reported as being too ill and too melancholy (and too bad tempered) to do any of his regular business or meet any ambassadors. He was said to suffer from gout in every part of his body, hemorrhoids, and catarrh so bad that he could not speak or, if he spoke, could not be heard. But from the privacy of his apartments in Brussels from which he rarely stirred (for he was indeed so ill that he sometimes had to get his sister to write his letters for him), Charles worked out his strategy.

Even before it was clear that Mary would be victorious, the Emperor had doubted whether his son Philip should continue with the negotiations then under way for him to marry the Portuguese Princess Maria. On June 23, from the precise and detailed instructions he sent his ambassadors in England, it is clear that he knew exactly what his objective was. Mary in her initial enthusiasm and reformatory zeal was not to proceed in haste on any matter. She was to make no immediate changes in government or religious affairs, in case they should interfere with the marriage he had in view for her. She was to be told to dissemble and if necessary agree to marry an Englishman. Time, the Emperor thought, would then help her to achieve her real aims. And the unwanted suitors (from his point of view) could be set at variance with each other while negotiations went ahead with the preferred one. A little later he was again writing on the same subject to brief Renard in his tactics: once Mary was firmly on the throne, her thoughts should be directed toward the necessity of marriage; after she was convinced, "steps will be taken towards the Councillors and others so that this affair may be decorously conducted, as is suitable in all that concerns her."[15] In other words, the Councillors were to be bribed secretly, but on the surface it was to look as though Mary was behaving in her usual modest manner in all that concerned her personally.

The first suggestion to Philip that he should make Mary his wife was broached by Charles in a letter to his son, dated July 30, 1553, and written as soon as he had heard the news that Mary had been proclaimed Queen. Philip immediately wrote back to agree, though because of the war with France, communications were such that his father did not receive his assent until September 11. For the Emperor, the marriage was a symbol of his plan to encircle France by wedding England to the Netherlands. If there had been no other way, he himself would have been willing to marry his cousin in order to bring about this objective. "I am sure," he wrote, perhaps not entirely accurately, "that if the English made up their minds to accept a foreigner, they would more readily accept me than any other, for they have always shown a liking for me."[16] But at his age and in his state of health, the sacrifice was more than he cared to contemplate. He thought that Philip could be made acceptable in his place. He was fortunate in having a dutiful son who, ignoring the vanity of his father, was willing to agree. The Emperor's problems were Philip's insofar as the territories over which he governed were concerned.

With Mary the situation was more complex.
First, there was her formidable conscience with which
he had to deal. Mary took her duties toward her people
seriously. She wanted to do what was best for them
regardless of her own wishes as a private individual. She
confessed to Renard "that she had never felt that which
was called love, nor harbored thoughts of voluptuous-
ness, and had never considered marriage until God had
been pleased to raise her to the throne."[17] Renard,
carrying out his master's instructions, explained to Mary
the advantages of marriage including "that she might be
relieved of pains and travail which were rather men's
work than of the profession of ladies."[18] Not till October 10, did the Emperor himself write to Mary to suggest openly that she should marry. "As we believe that
one of the greatest benefits that might be conferred on
the country would be that you should have posterity to
succeed you, we are obliged by our brotherly affection
to tell you that whatever determination you may have
come to before you acceded, you must now consider
accepting some aspirant who shall be agreeable to yourself and profitable to the Kingdom; and the sooner you
make up your mind the better."[19] He made no mention
of Philip, but before Mary had received the letter, Renard had already suggested to her the possibility of her
marrying the Emperor's son.

It was not too difficult for Mary to give up the
idea of chastity imposed, or encouraged, by her mother
and her unhappy early life. The idea too may not have
been altogether displeasing that she might bear children—not only for her own sake but also because she
might thereby displace Elizabeth from the succession
envisaged by Henry VIII. But it was no easy task to
convince her that the marriage to Philip would be acceptable to her subjects. The hatred of the English for
foreigners was well known and had been instrumental in

preventing all previous attempts to find her a husband from being successful. With her usual inability to make a decision for herself, Mary leaned heavily both on the Emperor, through his ambassador Renard, and on a few select members of the Council, chief among whom were Gardiner, Paget, Arundel, Petre, the Bishop of Norwich (Thomas Thirlby) and Rochester. But the advice Mary received was conflicting. Paget (who had specialized in Imperial affairs under Somerset) was without difficulty flattered and bribed by Renard into becoming Philip's advocate. He begged her to regard the marriage as a solemn alliance which might be of the greatest advantage to her kingdom and subjects, bringing peace and security to all. His words were offset by those who denigrated Philip's character, reiterated that as a foreigner he would never be acceptable to the English people, and asserted that marriage to him would embroil England in the Emperor's wars against France and in his struggles with his own subjects.

Mary hesitated, torturing herself with her own indecisiveness. She wept. She prayed. She spent sleepless nights trying to make up her mind. Once it was made up nothing was going to change it. But the question now was which of the possible suitors would best please her people. She felt she could not marry one of her own subjects, so that eliminated Courtenay who had also shown himself to be unsatisfactory on other grounds. Reginald Pole had eliminated himself. The other foreign candidates—among whom were the Archduke Ferdinand (nephew of Charles V and son of the ruler of the Austrian portion of the Hapsburg Empire), and Don Luis of Portugal, more eager for marriage now that Mary was Queen than when she had been only the illegitimate half-sister of the King—were equally unacceptable. Not only were they foreign, but the Emperor

had indicated that he did not approve of them. Neither
they nor Mary would have gone against his wishes.

Courtenay was the favorite of the English people, of Gardiner and of the three gentlemen of Mary's
household who had always been her staunch supporters
in times of stress—Rochester, Inglefield and Wal-
degrave. The French and Venetians also supported him
if only because they feared the repercussions of a per-
manent English-Hapsburg alliance. Courtenay himself,
an ambitious but frivolous young man, was not against
the proposal but had not the slightest idea of how to
cope with the superior intellects against which he was
pitted. De Noailles used every diplomatic weapon he
possessed. He spread rumors. He encouraged any
movement which could be used against the marriage.
No means were beneath him to secure his objective. De
Noailles invoked the specter of the Inquisition. He
needled Courtenay and encouraged him and Elizabeth in
their rebellious thoughts. Neither was unwilling to be
used. Both were vain and ambitious. And Elizabeth did
not have the same loyalty, was not moved by the same
scruples in regard to her sister that Mary had had in
regard to Edward VI. According to Renard, "the Lady
Elizabeth is greatly to be feared for she has a power of
enchantment."[20] Mary was aware that Courtenay and
Elizabeth were both openly and secretly in contact with
the French and Venetian ambassadors. But there was
not much she could do to prevent such meetings. Elizabeth chafed under the close surveillance kept on her
movements and wanted to leave court for one of her
own houses. Eventually, at the end of the year, Mary
gave her permission to depart. Renard did not agree.
He would rather she had been sent to the Tower. The
instructions he had received about Courtenay, however,
were to be cautious. If the marriage with Philip turned

out not to be possible, Courtenay was the Emperor's next favorite candidate.

Both Charles V and Henry II were experts at planting seeds of new ideas or seeds of doubts in other people's minds. It is fascinating to read their instructions to their ambassadors—who were also expert at carrying out such instructions. The Emperor had first feigned not to want the Spanish marriage more than any other advantageous to England. Neither Mary nor her Council were to be brutally faced with his true aims, but gently brought round to accept them. He was fortunate in having so able a negotiator as his new young ambassador, Renard, who almost equalled his master in his skill at putting across a point. His subtle blend of flattery, suggestion and logic combined with his shrewd judgment of character won him many an argument. The memorandum he sent to Mary about her marriage was a model of lucid and precise exposition, especially when compared with Pole's on religion.* Even so, it took all the Emperor's cunning and his ambassador's rhetoric to win over first Mary and then her Council.

In the latter attempt they were aided by Paget who, thinking to make use of Gardiner's disapproval of the marriage in order to advance his own position, took the arrangements into his own hands as far as he was able. He gave valuable advice. He knew which arguments would be used against the marriage and so could help Renard to counter them before they were advanced. He also knew which members of the Council could be counted on to be helpful and which could be safely ignored. He provided six names of members to whom the Emperor wrote to ask for cooperation.** But Paget also showed some regard for Mary's welfare. "The

*See page 136.
**The Chancellor, the Bishop of Durham, the Earl of Shrewsbury, Sir Robert Rochester, Lord Paget, and Sir William Petre.

Queen's happiness ought to be taken into consideration, as well as her age and comfort."[21] He had heard that Philip spoke no other language but Spanish. "If the marriage were to come off, it would be expedient for him to learn to speak and understand English, otherwise it would prove a dumb marriage, and he could hold no communication with Council or with the people."[22]

At last Mary made up her mind. On Sunday, October 29, she called Renard to her at New Hall and swore before the Holy Sacrament that she would marry Philip. Then, having made her decision, she became her old stubborn self, meeting all resistance to her will with authority. The news was not immediately made public. The Council first had to be informed in such a way that they would also approve. Especially the Chancellor, Courtenay's advocate, had to be convinced. Gardiner proved to be almost as stubborn as Mary and did not give in easily. He listed all the obstacles to the marriage: the hatred of the Spanish character which existed not only in England but also in other parts of the Emperor's domains, for Philip's manner had already displeased the Flemish, the Italians and the Germans; the likelihood of becoming involved in the Emperor's war with the French (who were already allied to Scotland) and the inherent dangers of such a situation; the dispensation from the Pope which would be necessary for cousins to be able to marry (though this would have to be kept secret as the English people would not tolerate that the Pope should be consulted); the fact that Philip did not speak English; the dangers to his person if he came to England.

Point by point and at length Renard refuted his objections until Gardiner gave in, saying that if the Queen wished to marry a foreigner he would not demur. Renard hurriedly sent off a jubilant letter to acquaint Philip with the good news and to advise him to practice speaking French or Latin in anticipation of his arrival in England (Renard was not so optimistic as to expect Philip to master the English language). Gardiner was never really won over, but he kept quiet after having confessed to Mary with tears in his eyes that he had grown fond of Courtenay when they were in the Tower together. Mary somewhat drily asked him whether it would be suitable to force her "to marry a man because the Bishop had conceived a friendship for him in prison."[23]

A delegation from Parliament came to see Mary in order to plead Courtenay's case "and to set forth all the disadvantages, dangers and difficulties that could be imagined or dreamed of in the case of her choosing a foreign husband."[24] Mary was offended and angry. She answered them with a forceful and reasoned argument, finally silencing them by saying that "all her affairs had been conducted by divine disposition, so she would pray God to counsel and inspire her in her choice of a husband who should be beneficial to the Kingdom and agreeable to herself."[25]

In the end, her trust in God and the Emperor again proved to have been misplaced. For the time being however it seemed as though God was indeed on her side, for the opposition to the marriage had been silenced, and the Emperor seemed about to have his efforts rewarded. But Charles had not reckoned with the English people. He had assumed their approval would follow that of the Council. He had underestimated the depth of their feeling against a foreign marriage and overestimated Mary's (and Renard's) ability to assess that feeling.

When Mary had been reassured that Philip was free to marry her (no Portuguese betrothal had taken place), that he wanted to marry her, that he was indeed "of even temper, of balanced judgment and well-conditioned" as she had been informed, and that Gardiner and the Council would not object, she wanted to press on with the arrangements for the marriage before any further obstacle could be raised. She said that Philip should come before Lent, otherwise the marriage could not take place until after Easter. Now that her mind was made up she was impatient of any delay. Perhaps too, remembering her age, she wanted to lose no time if there was to be issue from the marriage. She told Renard that he had so convinced her of His Highness's good qualities that she had already fallen in love with him, then added with a characteristic touch of humor, that His Highness might not be obliged to Renard for it.

Mary hoped that the Queen of Hungary might visit her, as she was anxious to make her acquaintance. But because of the situation in Brussels and the health of the Emperor, the Queen replied that she did not expect to be able to come over until Philip arrived in England. Mary also expressed a desire to see Philip before the marriage, but this was not practicable either. Perhaps Renard, the same age as Philip, thought it better too that they should not meet until it was too late for either to turn back. Instead, they exchanged portraits. Mary sent one painted by Sir Anthony Mor (Antonio Moro). The Emperor's sister sent one of Philip "that was painted three years ago by Titian and was considered a very good likeness by everybody at that time. It is true that the portrait has suffered a little from time ... but it will serve to tell her what he is like, if she will put it in a proper light and look at it from a distance, as all Titian's paintings have to be looked at. She will of course know that the likeness is no longer exact ... and she will be able to imagine, from what he was then, the progress he will have made in the last three years."[26] What Mary, being nearsighted, was able to make of the portrait is not recorded.

The marriage articles were drawn up in Brussels but with Paget's connivance, for he knew what could be made acceptable to the Council and what could not. At the end of the year the Emperor sent to London a large delegation consisting of three noble envoys led by the Count of Egmont,* supported by some four hundred other people, for the "knitting up of the marriage of the Queen."[27] The attendants were pelted with snowballs by the boys in the streets, but the reception given to the ambassadors by the Council was more hospitable. On January 2, they arrived at the Tower of London where they were ceremoniously welcomed. A week later they formally requested Mary's hand in marriage for Philip, Prince of Spain. The Queen, in apparent modesty, refused to speak on so delicate a matter as her own marriage. But she knew what she was doing. She deliberately left it to her Council to give the assent. The terms of the marriage treaty proved acceptable to both Houses of Parliament. It seemed, therefore, that nothing remained except for the marriage articles to be signed by both parties and for Philip to come to England to wed his bride.

This proved not to be the case. All the provisos in the wedding treaty were not enough to ensure its success with the English people. They did not care one way or the other about the terms of the treaty. It was the marriage itself that disturbed them. There had been foreign marriages suggested for Mary before but nothing had ever come of them, whereas this one was serious and about to take place in the near future. Already in November, when news of Mary's decision had leaked, there had been signs of unrest. Now popular opinion

---

*Egmont later became a Protestant and a revolutionary hero in the Netherlands and was made the subject of a play by Goethe with accompanying music by Beethoven.

was further excited by the spreading of rumors—that Edward VI was still alive; that the Spaniards were already on their way in large numbers to take over England; and all the old religious bogeys were revived. The public announcement of the marriage was the signal for rebellion.

# 4. Rebellion

The rebellion was limited to the southern, more Protestant, part of the country. The original intention had been that it should break out in several places at the same time. But it had not been possible to keep the movement secret, and communication between the different sectors was difficult. Gardiner summoned Courtenay who, not renowned for his courage, half-confessed and was sent to the Tower. The other leaders, in some confusion, plunged in desperately only to be defeated one by one. Sir Peter Carew in the southwest, the Duke of Suffolk in the Midlands, and Sir James Croft on the Welsh border were easily overcome by Mary's loyal forces. Carew escaped to France; Suffolk and Croft were captured.

In the southeast it was more complicated. Fifteen thousand Kentish men were said to have rallied to Sir Thomas Wyatt (son of the poet who had once been in love with Elizabeth's mother, Anne Boleyn). He claimed not to be fighting for Elizabeth and Courtenay, but against Mary's foreign marriage and the Catholic religion. (The two issues were always confused in people's minds.) Five hundred Londoners set out against them, clad in white coats with red crosses—the uniform which was taken from the English flag and worn by citizens trained to fight in time of need. When they met, however, most of the white coats joined the rebels. To-

gether they marched on London, where the panic-
stricken inhabitants prepared to withstand them. The
gates were manned by soldiers in armor and the Tower
was filled with supplies.

The Council were divided among themselves and
therefore useless. At first Mary was bewildered, especially as she had few men-at-arms about her whom
she could trust. But she was unafraid. She went by boat
from Westminster to the Guild Hall. There she made a
long and moving speech which had the result of replacing the fear and terror in men's hearts with courage and
enthusiasm for their Queen. She spoke openly of Wyatt
and his cause and his desire to take the Tower of
London, "the strongest bulwark of the kingdom with
the whole treasure of the realm and all arms which are
kept there,"[28] how wrong he was and how she would be
pleased to submit again the whole matter to Parliament.
If the marriage were to be found contrary to the advantage of the country she would not pursue it. As she had
remained single the best part of her life she would
rather renounce the marriage than that her people
should fight one another.

> I say to you on the word of a prince, I cannot tell how
> naturally the mother loveth the child, for I was never
> the mother of any, but certainly if a prince and governor
> may as naturally and earnestly love her subjects, as the
> mother doth love her child, then assume yourselves that
> I, being your lady mistress, do as earnestly and tenderly
> love and favor you. . . . And now good subjects, pluck up
> your hearts like true men, stand fast against these reb-
> els, both our enemies and yours, and fear them not, for I
> assure you I fear them nothing at all.[29]

Mary ordered all bridges over the Thames in the neighborhood of London to be destroyed, as much to prevent
untrustworthy elements from leaving to join the rebels

*Sir Thomas Wyatt, son of the poet. Leader of the ill-fated rebellion of 1554. Surrendered and was sent to the Tower where he was beheaded the same year. (Artist unknown.) NATIONAL PORTRAIT GALLERY, LONDON.*

as Wyatt and his men from entering.* She offered a prize for the capture of Wyatt and a free pardon for all who abandoned him. She went back to Westminster and Whitehall, refusing to take refuge in the Tower or to go to Windsor where she could be protected more easily. The Emperor's emissaries hastily left the country, but

*In the case of London Bridge this meant raising the drawbridge, not destroying it.

Renard stayed by her side. He urged her not to leave London, saying that all would be lost if she went away: only her presence would keep her people loyal.

Wyatt's army was considerably reduced by the time it reached Southwark, across the Thames from London. Some had lost heart for the cause itself. Others had had their enthusiasm dampened by the muddy state of the roads they had marched along, and by the wintry weather. When they found they could not cross the river, they worked off some of their frustration by wreaking a certain amount of damage in the neighborhood, including the destruction of Gardiner's library. Marching upstream on the south bank, with London so tantalizingly in view and out of reach, they arrived at Kingston. According to one report, the bridge here was only partially destroyed; Wyatt and a few of his men swam across the river and were able to repair the bridge sufficiently for the rest to cross over on it. According to another story, they found the ferry boats on their side of the river and used them to make their crossing. What is sure is that Wyatt's army, said by this time to number some 7,000 men, now had no obstacle between them and their objective. The way to London was clear and their aim was the City where they expected to be given a rousing welcome.

Again there was panic in London, with Mary one of the few people to remain calm. The fight began early in the morning of Ash Wednesday, February 7. By midday the rebels were in the field of St. James near Westminster. Mary did not ride at the head of her troops inciting them to victory, as her grandmother Isabella was said to have done. She prayed constantly and encouraged those around her by keeping calm in her certitude of winning. Even so, not everybody shared her confidence or wanted her to win. The situation was tense as Wyatt and his troops neared Hyde Park Corner. But

Mary's loyal soldiers were still numerous and their leaders astute. When the opposing forces met, the Queen's men opened up and deliberately let Wyatt and a few hundred of his men get through. Then they closed their ranks. Wyatt's army was successfully divided. Thereafter there was confusion among those left behind. It was difficult to tell who was friend and who was foe. Mary could have been in considerable danger, but the invaders were leaderless and in all the turmoil made no move toward Westminster. They were set upon by the Earl of Pembroke's men who slew some, took many prisoners and dispersed the rest. Mary's ladies were terrified both of the soldiers outside the gates and of the loyal armed men in the Queen's presence chamber. Mary was unafraid and rallied her palace retainers from a balcony before coming down to join them.

Meanwhile Wyatt approached the City by way of Charing Cross with barely three hundred tired men behind him. When he reached the gate he called out and asked to be let in by those he thought were his friends. He was refused admission. He started to retrace his footsteps, uncertain what to do. Halted by the Queen's troops, he had then no choice but to surrender; he was sent to the Tower before 4:00 p.m. on that same day. In spite of reports to the contrary, less than one hundred of Wyatt's followers were killed in all. It was said that the Queen's men shot their arrows in the air rather than at their supposed enemies. "The noise of women and children, when the conflict was at Charing Cross, was so great and shrill, that it was heard to the top of the White Tower."[30] The prisoners in the Tower can have known little of the progress of the battle, though they were probably not unaware that it was taking place. Until that time it was likely that Jane Grey would shortly have been freed in spite of her condemnation in November, but her father's involvement in the insurrection was her death knell. It was also said he had again proclaimed her Queen at Leicester. Her family had been implicated too often in traitorous exploits and she had the misfortune to be their chief instrument.

The day after Wyatt's arrest, Mary signed the death warrant of Jane and her husband. Mary would still have spared them, but she was overruled by the Council. In her last days Jane made a detailed statement of all that had happened to her since the death of Edward VI. She admitted "lack of prudence" but hoped for clemency from the Queen as all that had been done had been done "without her fault or agreement." When a theologian was sent to convert her to Catholicism, she countered argument with argument. Finally she thanked him for his company but let him know that she was more bored by his presence than frightened by the shadow of death. On February 12, 1554, Guilford Dudley was beheaded in public on Tower Green and then his wife Jane Grey met the same fate privately (because she was of royal blood) in the precincts of the Tower.

Mary has been blamed for sending Jane to her death. The true blame, however, lies not with Mary, but with all those people who used Jane as their instrument to further their own ambition. It was not even Northumberland who was most responsible, but Jane's own father. This time he did not go free. He was arraigned on a charge of high treason in Westminster Hall and condemned to death. Twelve days after his daughter, he too was beheaded.

Mary had been urged to realize the danger of clemency in a world used to harsh measures. As a result, about sixty of those who had taken part in the Wyatt uprising met their end on gallows set up at all the gates of London and in many public places. Some were taken back to Kent so that the spectacle of their execution would serve as a lesson to other would-be rebels. But about four hundred others were pardoned.* Wyatt, as the ringleader, was condemned to be hanged, drawn and quartered, but his sentence was not carried out immediately in the hope that he might implicate others. Before his execution, which did not take place until April 12, he accused both Courtenay and Elizabeth of conspiracy. There was, however, a report that he withdrew his accusation when faced with his death on the scaffold.

Courtenay was already in the Tower as a prisoner. Elizabeth had also been implicated by a letter that fell into the hands of the Council. She had been summoned to court when the rebellion was first reported, but had delayed her arrival for some time by pleading illness. Various reasons were offered for her failure to appear at court, probably the most scurrilous being the one (reported by Renard) that she was pregnant—accompanied by unnecessary aspersions on characteristics inherited from her mother Anne Boleyn. On February 22, Elizabeth arrived in London "dressed all in white. She had her litter opened to show herself to the people and her pale face kept a proud, haughty expression in order to mask her vexation"[31] (said Renard who, it must be remembered, was not describing this scene altogether objectively). On arrival, her personal staff was cut down to one gentleman, three ladies and two servants. She was kept under close supervision in the Queen's Palace with guards outside her window and in her antechamber.

When Elizabeth was examined, she denied any involvement in the rebellion, but the evidence was strong against her. Mary hesitated to send her to the Tower, knowing that there were many in authority who secretly supported her. She asked her Council which one of them would be willing to have Elizabeth in his

---

*Renard thought it would have been better if they had all been executed instead of setting them at liberty to strengthen Elizabeth's party.

house. Nobody was willing to take the risk of being compromised. On March 18, therefore, Elizabeth was despatched to the Tower. When she was tried she firmly denied all charges. The Emperor (and Renard—who was perhaps a little bewitched by her and over-anxious to remove her) advised that she should be executed. Mary for once was firm against their advice, determined not to go against the law of her country. Her first Parliament had restored the law by which treason must be proved before any English person could be convicted, and the evidence against Elizabeth was not conclusive. Although she herself also believed Elizabeth to be guilty, she did not allow herself to be guided by personal prejudice. Elizabeth was kept in the Tower for two months with Sir Henry Bedingfield as her guard and protector. When Mary released Elizabeth to go to her house at Woodstock in Oxfordshire, Bedingfield accompanied her. A few days later Courtenay was also released to house arrest at Fotheringhay.

After the suppression of the Wyatt rebellion, the French and Venetian ambassadors, denying by their attitude any complicity in the abortive plot, came to congratulate Mary and the Council on the Queen's fortunate escape. Mary was not deceived by their words. A close watch was still kept on their movements, of which they were not unaware, and they did not hesitate to complain.

Renard had earlier expressed some doubt as to whether it would be safe for Philip to come to England when the Council and the country were so divided. Mary had burst into tears. She swore that she would do all she could to conciliate her subjects and bring order to her realm. She considered removing herself from London to Yorkshire, where she would be safer in a more Catholic community. Thinking of the loss of prestige and the drop in profitable commerce that would ensue if the Sovereign departed, the citizens petitioned the Queen to stay, promising to approve her marriage if she did so. But their behavior belied their words. Innumerable pamphlets were circulated aginst the Queen and her religion and Elizabeth's name was constantly associated with the agitators. A curious incident was reported by Renard to the Emperor: "When I had nearly finished this letter, I heard that the heretics had put up a man and a woman in a house here in London to rouse the people by asserting that a voice was to be heard in a wall, and it was the voice of an angel. When they said to it, 'God save Queen Mary!' it answered not; but when they said, 'God save the Lady Elizabeth!' the voice replied, 'So be it!'"[32] He went on to say that the fraud had so much success that by eleven in the morning there were over 17,000 people collected round the house.

## 5. *Philip Comes to England*

The Count of Egmont and his fellow ambassadors had returned to England in March, primed with the latest advice from the Emperor and carrying a copy of the marriage treaty which the Emperor had endorsed. They were empowered to stand in for Philip in the betrothal ceremony which took place on March 6 in Mary's palace of Whitehall. Egmont placed on Mary's finger a costly ring sent by the Emperor on behalf of his son. A few days later he left for Spain to help Philip prepare for his journey.

Renard was still extremely worried about Philip's safety and not satisfied by the assurances given to him by the Queen and her Council that they would see that he was in no danger. He sent to the Emperor an assessment of the position as he saw it:

I have lately been turning over in my mind the state of affairs of this kingdom. Religion is unsettled, the Queen's own Councillors are at odds, the nobility and the people hate one another, and the English temper is fickle, treacherous and unfaithful, naturally hostile to strangers, prone to discord at home, now inflamed against the Spaniards by French incitement.... On the other hand, it is more important that his Highness's person, on whom the hopes of so many kingdoms, countries and peoples repose, should be safeguarded, and it is so difficult to put any trust in the English....[33]

The Emperor, however, was not to be deflected from his purpose. Renard was told not to frighten Philip or delay him further by telling him too much about the situation in England. But Philip knew enough to want to be kept informed and to delay his departure until he had enough ships ready to carry a large number of supporting Spaniards. "Our household and court will contain about 3000 persons, not counting the men who are going to guard the fleet, for they will be 6000 over and above the sailors."[34] Mary's warning to him to bring his own cooks and physicians can have done little to reassure him.

On April 12, Parliament met in London and the Royal Marriage Bill was passed by both Houses. But agreement had not been obtained without some cost to the Emperor. He not only had his own large representational staff to support; he had to maintain and increase his fleet in order for it to be strong enough to safeguard Philip's voyage through French-infested seas. He also had to provide large sums of money to reward those in England who had been helpful and buy off those who were opposed. "More is to be done with money here than in any other country in the world,"[35] said Egmont. And a few days later, a dispatch from all the ambassadors said: "We consider it our duty to inform your Majesty that they [the English] would think nothing of a small present, but disdain it.... It would be better to make no gifts at all rather than alienate, by an inconsiderable offering, the sincere affection for your Majesty and his Highness which they have so far displayed."[36]

There was some dispute between the Emperor and Renard about the best way of distributing their largesse. Renard wanted it to be given before Philip's arrival in order to smooth the Prince's way and perhaps give more prestige to the ambassador. The Emperor thought it better for Philip to bring the bribes (or rewards) with him in order to achieve the same purpose but give the prestige to his son. In the end money was provided for both. But Mary's request for a loan, of which she was desperately in need, was ignored. She was even more than usually short of money as the rebellion, either by design or intent, had blocked her access to her usual sources of revenue.

After Mary's betrothal in front of witnesses and the agreement of Parliament to the marriage articles, Philip had no further excuse to delay his departure. But Philip was in no hurry. He was hardly an ardent suitor. During all the negotiations he had never written directly to Mary or sent her presents, and she was far from happy about this state of affairs. Renard had to comfort her and write at her request a postscript to one of his letters to Philip. He sent Mary's greetings and apologized for her not writing but "as she had not yet received letters from you it was not for a lady to begin." He continued, "She finds the time long, and asks continually when you will come."[37]

Mary was, however, too impatient to keep her ladylike silence. Later in April she sent by Renard's messenger a restrained letter with only a hint of rebuke in it.

> Although you have not privately written to me since our
> alliance has been negotiated, so it is that, feeling myself
> so much obliged by the sincere and true affection which
> you bear me, which you have so much confirmed by
> deeds, as by the letters written to the said ambassador
> ... I could not omit signifying to you my good wishes
> and duty which I have ever to communicate to you....
> And hoping shortly to supply the remainder verbally, I
> will make an end at present....

She signed herself "Your entirely assured and most
obliged Ally, Mary."[38]

Philip had never shown any great enthusiasm for
the marriage. After he had dutifully agreed to do what
his father considered best for the Empire, he took his
time over the formalities. "For the love of God appear
to be pleased,"[39] wrote the Emperor's ambassador in
Rome. Slightly more gracefully, his aunt the Queen of
Hungary wrote, "I trust in God that He has endowed
you with sufficient gifts and will give you His grace to
acquit yourself of the task to your own credit and the
honor of your realms."[40] His father also had some mis-
givings. To the Duke of Alva, who was to accompany
Philip to England, Charles wrote an urgent postscript:
"Duke, for the love of God, see to it that my son be-
haves in the right manner; for otherwise I tell you I
would rather never have taken the matter in hand at
all."[41] But in spite of doubts about both his son's tact
and his son's real desire to marry and to live in England,
Charles continually urged him to press on with his journey. The Emperor was no more moved by affection for
Philip than he was by affection for Mary in his efforts to
promote the union.

Philip had empowered the Emperor's ambassadors in London to swear to observe the articles of the
marriage treaty on his behalf; but he had also registered
a legal protest, in much the same spirit that Mary had

signed her capitulation to Henry VIII. Before witnesses in Valladolid, "he protested once, twice and thrice, or as many times as it was necessary to make the act legal, and to ensure that the power and confirmation that he was about to grant should be invalid and without force to bind him." He said that he had never of his own free will agreed, and never would agree, to the articles. He would, however, agree to abide by them, as long as "it should forever be recorded, as a plain, clear and certain fact to stand as long as the world should last"[42] that he had given his oath in order that the marriage might take place and not of his own free will.

Whether the Emperor ever saw this document or whether Mary was ever aware of its contents is not known. Only one sentence in a letter Charles sent to his son suggests that he and Mary knew something of Philip's real feelings. When writing of the need for Philip to ratify the marriage articles speedily, he added, "The Queen, however, assures us that in secret it shall be done according to your desire."[43]

In May Philip appears to have had a change of heart, whatever may have been his motives. He wrote almost tenderly of Mary to Renard: "When news of the rebellion began to arrive here, I was most anxious and grieved for the Queen's sake.... You will always send me good news of her and her health; for you know how much pleasure it gives me to receive them."[44] He also sent her a valuable jewel, "a great diamond set in a rose," which had once been given to his mother by his father. He congratulated Renard and graciously acknowledged his exertions that showed him to be "a zealous minister in his Majesty's and our service."

He left Valladolid on May 12, on the first stage of his journey toward England. He travelled slowly and by easy stages, stopping to transact various pieces of business on the way, which pleased neither his father nor his

*Philip II of Spain, son of the Emperor Charles V. Married Mary in November 1554. Although he was called King of England out of courtesy, he was never crowned. (Artist unknown.)* NATIONAL PORTRAIT GALLERY, LONDON.

bride. But he had a legitimate excuse: as Prince of Spain he had responsibilities toward his country. He had also arranged to meet his sister Juana, who was to act as Regent during his absence, but she was ill and he was delayed waiting for her arrival from Portugal. And he can hardly be blamed for going to say farewell to his old grandmother Juana, who could rarely have been given the privilege of seeing him or any other visitor. Although by title joint ruler of Spain with her son Charles V, she had now spent some forty years shut away in her castle at Tordesillas.

It also took time to prepare Philip's large retinue and to assemble the fleet of ships to carry them. Renard had suggested that a small number of followers might be more acceptable to the English, to which Philip's reply was that his own desire would have been to set out accompanied only by his own normal household, but that would have diminished his prestige, let alone the necessity of going well-prepared. He had also to be ready to cope with a possible French attack by sea, as well as a possible stormy reception by the English on land. For that reason it was suggested to him that, as no Spanish soldiers should be seen to land in England, he should resort to a stratagem.[45] His nobles should dress their soldiers in the same liveries as their pages and lackeys, and their weapons should be stowed in the chests in which they carried their belongings. The nobles themselves could bear arms openly because of the war in progress between the Empire and France.

At last Philip arrived on the Spanish coast. On Thursday, July 12, his fleet set sail from Corunna. It consisted of eighty large ships and up to one hundred and twenty smaller caravels. About forty other ships waited for soldiers that had not arrived. The journey through the Bay of Biscay was rough and made Philip too seasick to cope with any business, but the rest of the journey was calm. The following Tuesday they caught their first glimpse of England "with no little contentment." The next day they met and exchanged salvos with the eighteen English and eighteen Flemish galleons which had been idling in the waters between the Isle of Wight and Southampton for some two months awaiting the arrival of the Spanish ships. Indeed they had been waiting so long that the Flemish ships had begun to run out of provisions and the English sailors had shown signs of mutiny. The Emperor's Vice-Admiral sought permission to revictual, having been told that food was cheap in England, but this turned out to be no longer true. The enterprise and greed of the local inhabitants had driven them to take advantage of the situation by putting up their prices. The Emperor's sister sent a large sum of money to cover the cost of the revictualling, with instructions to borrow if what she had sent was not enough. The Imperial ships should not disappear from English waters, she said, "for so petty a reason at the very time when the Prince's coming is looked for."[46]

## 6. The Wedding

On July 19, exactly one year after Mary's proclamation, Philip arrived in the waters off Southampton, the city chosen for his reception because of its predominantly Catholic population which could be counted upon to behave. He immediately sent messengers to inform the Queen of his arrival and then waited, no doubt in some trepidation, for the ceremonies of welcome to begin. The next day, Renard, de Courrières and eight English noblemen came on board. In the name of the Queen, Philip was decorated with the Order of the Garter. Then he was invited to come on the Queen's

*Mary and Philip in 1554, the year of their marriage. (Artist unknown.) BY KIND PERMISSION OF THE MARQUESS AND MARCHIONESS OF TAVISTOCK.*

barge, festively trimmed with the Tudor colors of green and white. Philip accepted graciously, outwardly at any rate, showing confidence in his hosts. Most of his followers were directed to Portsmouth, some ten miles away, to disembark. Philip's command was that no soldiers or horses were to come ashore. They were to wait until after the wedding when both fleets would set sail to go to the assistance of the Emperor, who had just lost two important fortresses to the French.

On landing in Southampton, Philip was greeted by Gardiner and a brilliant company of English nobles and was given as a present from Mary a horse decked with crimson velvet embroidered with gold and pearls. Dressed in his customary black with a short Spanish cape over one shoulder, Philip mounted and rode off to the Church of the Holy Rood* to offer thanks for his safe arrival. In order to recuperate from his journey, he stayed three days in the city, making every attempt to be civil and courteous, and adopting English habits even to the extent of drinking large quantities of ale (which was not his custom).

Meanwhile, in London, those in favor of the marriage had hoped that Philip's arrival would put an end to the unrest among those who were opposed: once Mary and Philip were married it would be too late to argue about the Queen's choice of husband and perhaps he would win over people by his charm. The long delay however gave the dissidents an opportunity for further agitation, which in turn created uncertainty among the rest. The Council was still divided but not on the same lines as before. Paget, who had done so much to promote the marriage, was now apparently conniving with Elizabeth, trying to ingratiate himself with her as insurance against the time when she should succeed if Mary

*The remains of this church are still to be seen in Southampton near the docks.

had no children. His disagreement with Gardiner had now become an open quarrel of such proportions that it outweighed his loyalty to Mary. And Gardiner lost no opportunity to blacken Paget to Mary, accusing him of being a heretic. The French had not given up their plan to use Elizabeth and Courtenay (who in the middle of May had been released from the Tower to house arrest). Mary was so worried and upset that she was persuaded to withdraw to Richmond for her greater personal security. She took with her some members of the Council, leaving others to cope with matters of state in London. Her potentially most dangerous opponents were sent to their country homes to keep them out of mischief.

Mary waited for news, ready to go toward Winchester directly she heard of Philip's arrival, but there was not a sign that he had yet left Spain. Renard was given lodgings in Richmond to be near her with advice. Two other ambassadors, de Courrières and Briviescade Munatones, had been sent by the Emperor, the former to lead the delegation, outranking Renard. Munatones, who had had long experience in dealing with disturbances created among and by Spaniards abroad, was to be in charge of civil and criminal jurisdiction in Philip's court in England. The Emperor foresaw that there could be trouble caused by ignorance of local manners and customs on the part of the new arrivals.

After two weeks, Mary moved from Richmond to Guildford and then to Farnham. When Renard heard that Philip was ready to leave Spain he went to Southampton to be ready to receive him. Mary stayed till she heard of Philip's arrival in England before leaving Farnham. She made her entry into Winchester on Friday, July 21, accompanied by all her court. She took up residence in the Bishop's Palace where again she waited—no doubt also in a state of great nervous tension—for Philip to join her.

Philip left Southampton on the twenty-third, accompanied by a hundred Englishmen wearing his livery and fewer than fifteen of his own countrymen. But the procession was joined by many who had come out of curiosity to see him so that by the time he reached Winchester, it numbered several thousand. Wrapped in a scarlet cloak, Philip travelled on horseback in a torrential downpour of rain which continued for the whole of his journey. He courteously refused when a messenger arrived from Mary urging him to turn back. After having been formally received by the Mayor and Aldermen, he went straight to a service in the cathedral conducted by Gardiner. He then proceeded to the Dean's House where he was to be lodged, which was not far from the Bishop's Palace. After he had changed and eaten supper, he was taken by a private way to see the Queen. For the first time Philip and Mary met face to face.

Coming to meet him at the door, Philip saw a small, thin middle-aged woman with a delicate frame. She wore a dress of black velvet with... a front of brocade embroidered with pearls and pearl seeds, a wimple of black velvet with a raised neckpiece of gold, and rich jewels on the hands and a girdle with diamonds and a band of the same."[47] Her aspect was grave and serious. Her face was round and well-formed, her complexion red and white, though a little wrinkled, her nose rather low and wide. Her hair was reddish and her eyes large and piercing, somewhat staring as she was very near-sighted. She gave the impression of having been a good-looking woman in her younger days. Her voice was loud and rough, almost like a man's, so that when she spoke she was heard a long way off.

Mary saw a short, slim, well-made young man of pale complexion. He had flaxen hair and thick fair eyebrows almost meeting over large blue eyes which found it hard to meet her gaze. His mouth was large with a

thick and drooping underlip. Whether he measured up
to his portrait did not matter; Mary was as prepared to
love the man as much as the idea she had formed of him.

They kissed each other according to the English
custom and then, in the presence of six aged gentlemen
of the English Council with as many ladies all dressed in
purple velvet, together with the Spanish gentlemen who
had accompanied Philip, they walked hand in hand to
two chairs under a richly decorated canopy. They spoke
in "courtly fashion" for one hour, he in Spanish and she
in French—and understood each other. The Queen, at
his request, taught him to say "goodnight" in English,
which he repeated to her attendants. She gave her hand
to kiss in the Spanish fashion to his gentlemen. The first
meeting was over and Philip returned to his own
apartments.

The following afternoon Mary and Philip met
officially for about fifteen minutes. In the evening, he
again made a private visit and Mary was formally told
that the Emperor had decided to make Philip a King in
his own right by bestowing upon him the kingdoms of
Naples and Jerusalem. Mary was very happy to hear the
news. She agreed with her Chancellor that the new title
should be proclaimed in church before the wedding ceremony. This time Philip stayed much longer and "when
he wanted to take leave he went to kiss the ladies in
attendance, among whom are few attractive and many
ugly ones."[48]

On Wednesday, July 25, the day of St. James the
patron saint of Spain, Philip and Mary were married
with pomp and glory in a ceremony which almost passed
description. Mary and the officials in charge had excelled themselves in their preparations—so that Philip
felt he could not wear one of the cloaks given to him
because it was too ornate ("a French robe of cloth of
gold, with the roses of England and pomegranates em-

broidered on it, adorned with drawn gold beads and seed pearls. The sleeves carry eighteen buttons, nine on each, made of table diamonds. The lining is of purple satin.")[49] Even so, he and his Spanish nobles* outdid in their attire the Queen and her Lords, who were "conspicuously dressed although not as richly as the Spaniards." Mary wore a dress of white satin, scarlet shoes and a mantle of cloth of gold studded with diamonds. In the middle of her breast she wore a big diamond which had been sent to her by Philip. Philip was clad in white leather doublet and hose embroidered with silver quills and a robe (also given to him by the Queen) of "drawn and fluted gold, very richly bestrewn with precious stones and pearls and a very rich sword of gold, black velvet cap with white feathers and a necklace that was sent to him by the Emperor."[50] He wore the Imperial Order of the Golden Fleece and also the blue ribbon of the English Order of the Garter. The Cathedral was resplendent with tapestries and cloth of gold. It was filled with spectators in magnificent attire —nobles, clerics, ambassadors—who watched the ceremony from eleven o'clock in the morning until three in the afternoon. Elizabeth, Courtenay, and de Noailles were conspicuously absent.**

Before the service began, de Figueroa presented a scroll to the Prince. The Prince read the scroll and presented it to the Queen who in turn handed it to the Chancellor. Gardiner, having also read it, then publicly proclaimed that the Emperor had presented his son with

---

*Including Juan de Figueroa, who reported the occasion.

**Although de Noailles was not present at the wedding he nevertheless was kept informed of all that happened. But what interested him more than the details of the ceremony was the number of soldiers who had accompanied Philip and when they were to move on to assist the Emperor in his fight against Henry II of France. He said that the citizens of London celebrated the marriage only under duress, but it is more likely that they were only too happy to be given the opportunity to enjoy free wine and food.

the kingdom of Naples and, he added, whereas "it was thought the Queen's Majesty should marry but with a prince, now it was manifested that she should marry with a King."[51] It was a nice theatrical touch on a theatrical occasion, and the Emperor could not have helped being pleased when he heard about it. More important was the reading out by de Figueroa of the marriage contract* which had been so carefully negotiated beforehand.

By this contract, Philip and Mary were to share equally the titles and honors possessed by both, their first titles being King and Queen of England. Philip was to share in the government of England with his wife, but it was stipulated that all rights, privileges and customs of the land should be maintained; no foreigners should be given public office; business should always be transacted in English; Philip should have no claim on English ships, armaments or treasure; and England should not be involved in the war between the Empire and France. If there were to be issue of the marriage, England would be ruled by the offspring according to English law; the oldest child would also inherit Burgundy and the Low Countries. If the Queen died before the King, the child or children were to stay in England and Philip would have no right to the accession. Philip's son by a previous marriage, Don Carlos, was to inherit Spain, Sicily, and Philip's other domains which Philip would inherit from Charles V.** If Don Carlos died without issue, his inheritance was to pass to the eldest child of Philip and Mary. If Philip died first, Mary was to receive a large sum of money.

---

*Only one chronicler mentions this. Another observer says that the marriage contract was held in Gardiner's hand but not read out.

**Part of the Empire was already governed by Charles's brother Ferdinand, who claimed the right to pass on that inheritance to his heirs.

The formalities over, Philip and Mary advanced further into the church and took up their positions. The banns were read in Latin and English, and the marriage was solemnized by the Chancellor. For her wedding ring, the Queen had chosen a simple loop of gold such as "maidens wore in the old time." After Mass had been sung, which lasted three hours, four heralds stepped forward. The chief of them then proclaimed their titles three times:

> The King and Queen Philip and Mary, by the Grace of God King and Queen of England, France, Naples, Jerusalem, Ireland, Defenders of the Faith, and Princes of Spain and Sicily, Archdukes of Austria, Dukes of Milan, Burgundy and Brabant, Counts of Hapsburg, Flanders and Tyrol.[52]

Nobody was likely to question at that moment how tenuous were their claims to some of these titles.

Philip and Mary came out of the Cathedral and walked hand in hand under a canopy of crimson velvet to the Palace, where a great banquet was held "more after the English than the Spanish fashion." There was music and dancing in which Philip and Mary took part, and the Winchester schoolboys came in and recited poems in praise of the marriage. At nine o'clock the festivities for that day were over, and "the Bishops blessed the bed with prayers and rites that have old been the custom of this realm."[53]

The following day Mary was not seen by anyone, according to English tradition. She took the opportunity to write to the Emperor to say "how happy the arrival of His Highness had made me, and to present to you my humble commendations and thanks for allying me with a Prince so full of virtues that the realm's honor and tranquillity will certainly be thereby increased."[54]

*London Bridge and the City of London in 1616, but much as it was in the sixteenth century, with shops on both sides. (From Visscher's VIEW OF LONDON.) FOLGER SHAKESPEARE LIBRARY, WASHINGTON, D.C.*

After a few days more in Winchester, Philip and Mary moved slowly toward London, staying in several places on the way. In Windsor Philip was installed as a Knight of the Garter. There was also a great public hunt. Their departure was delayed until August 5 because both Philip and Mary caught colds. Philip sent some of his Spanish attendants ahead as there was not going to be room for them in the places where the King and Queen were going to stay and the local inhabitants were making it difficult for Spaniards to find lodgings. Philip's Portuguese friend, Ruy Gomez, the Duke of Alva, Juan de Figueroa and three or four others accompanied him for the rest of his journey. The royal party came first to Richmond and then to Southwark. On August 19 the King and Queen made their state entry into the City over London Bridge— "built of stone with twenty arches, and shops on both sides." They were greeted with the usual pageants and decorations, similar to those arranged for Mary's coronation. The cheering crowds gave no evidence of ill will, especially when they saw the carts of bullion which Philip had brought with him and which formed part of the procession. Philip and Mary stayed in Whitehall Palace for a few days before moving out of London to Hampton Court, which became their principal residence.

# CHAPTER VI

# KING PHILIP AND QUEEN MARY

## 1. Early Difficulties

Mary could not have known much about Philip's past history and his idiosyncrasies before her marriage. Nor could she have been as objective a judge of his character, or he of hers, as the Venetian ambassadors who described them both. Philip was said to be very like the Emperor in appearance, in habits and in mode of life, imitating his father's benign and gracious ways and actions. But unlike his father, who had been brought up in Flanders and spoke mainly French, he was very Spanish in speech, in outlook and in his court etiquette, which was extremely formal and dignified. He did not share the Emperor's liking for military pursuits being, by contrast to the Emperor when young, rather languid and taking little or no exercise. Already his health was troubling him, and he was said to be particularly subject to bowel complaints, which affected his choice of diet. He was grave and serious, polite and courteous, slow in speech and movement. He was very religious and studious, particularly of history, and was patient and assiduous in his attention to business. He was a man of few words at all times, but he listened carefully and his answers were short and to the point. He rarely looked anyone in the eye when conversing, either keeping his eyes down or allowing them to wander. He spoke only in Spanish, though he understood Latin and could speak a little; he also understood some French and Italian.[1]

Judging by what we already know about Mary, the Venetian descriptions of her at this time ring true:

> She is not of strong constitution, and of late she suffers from headaches and serious affection of the heart so that she is often obliged to take medicine and also to be blooded. She is of very spare diet and never eats until 1 p.m or 2 p.m. although she rises at daybreak, when, after saying her prayers and hearing Mass in private, she transacts business incessantly, until after midnight, when she retires to rest; for she chooses to give audience not only to all members of her Privy Council, and to hear from them every detail of public business, but also to all other persons who ask it of her. Her Majesty's countenance indicates great benignity and clemency, which are not belied by her conduct, for although she has had many enemies, and though so many of them were by law condemned to death, yet had the executions depended solely on her Majesty's will, not one of them perhaps would have been enforced. ... She is endowed with excellent ability, and more than moderately read in Latin literature, especially with regard to Holy Writ; and besides her native tongue she speaks Latin, French and Spanish, and understands Italian perfectly, but does not speak it. She is also very generous....
>
> Her Majesty takes pleasure in playing on the lute and the spinet, and is a very good performer on both instruments... But she seems to delight above all in arraying herself elegantly and magnificently. ... She also makes great use of jewels ... in which jewels she delights greatly, and although she has a great plenty of them left by her predecessors, yet were she better supplied with money than she is, she would doubtless buy many more.[2]

*Mary I*

Mary was also praised for the "quickness of her understanding, which comprehends whatever is intelligible to others, even to those who are not of her own sex (a marvellous gift for a woman)."[3]

A more jaundiced view was given by a "gentleman who accompanied the Prince to England and was present at all the ceremonies: 'The Queen is not at all beautiful: small and rather flabby than fat, she is of white complexion and fair, and has no eyebrows. She is a perfect saint, and dresses badly.'"[4] He goes on to describe the rest of the English women, who "wear petticoats of colored cloth without admixture of silk, and above come colored robes of damask, satin or velvet, very badly cut. Their shoes are sometimes of velvet, but more often of leather, and they wear black stockings and show their legs up to the knee when walking. As their skirts are not long they are passably immodest when walking, and even when seated. They are neither beautiful nor graceful when dancing, and their dances only consist in strutting or trotting about."[5]

Philip and Mary had many qualities in common and shared many of the same tastes. Both were ardent Catholics, serious and learned, melancholy by disposition, and admired for their virtue. Neither cared much for active sports and both liked dancing. Both were interested in the arts, Philip liking particularly sculpture and painting, Mary music. If Mary had been younger and Philip not the son of the Emperor, the marriage might conceivably have been a success. They differed in that Philip had been trained as a Prince, instructed by his father's advisers how to govern, and had been made Regent of Spain before he was sixteen. Mary was unschooled in the art of government, unsure of herself and therefore too dependent on the advice of others. She was not capable of dealing with her Privy Council and unruly countrymen on her own, even though she had shown herself to be extremely competent in times of stress. She could have used the advice which Charles V had given to his son in regard to his advisers: "make use of all but rely on none."

Philip was a man of the world. He had been married at sixteen to a cousin of approximately the same age, Maria of Portugal, who had died eighteen months later giving birth to their son Don Carlos. He had had a mistress since he was eighteen, to whom he had remained devoted until he came to England, when she was sent to a convent. In spite of her years, Mary was innocent and, by her own confession, had never been in love until now. Philip was prepared to be kind to Mary, and indeed was sufficiently attentive to please her and surprise the Emperor, who hoped he would continue to do so. Renard, perhaps with wishful thinking after all his labors had been brought to a successful conclusion, reported already in July that "the Queen is very happy with the King and the King with her."[6] And a month later, Philip's Portuguese friend Ruy Gomez wrote to another friend that the King "treats the Queen very kindly, and well knows how to pass over the fact that she is no good from the point of view of fleshly sensuality. He makes her so happy that the other day when they were alone she almost talked love talk to him and he replied in the same vein."[7]

Philip proved more affable and anxious to please in general than the English had been led to expect. He exerted his charm over some of the nobles so well that, with the assistance of the money he paid them, he apparently won their esteem and approval. His Spanish followers were not so fortunate. Philip had come to England with a Spanish household. On his arrival, he was also provided with an English household which he was expected to maintain. For a time he tried to run the two side by side, but without success. Jealousy and strife flourished and there was no fraternization. In addition, a large number of Spaniards had come to England in the hope of finding work. There were so many of them that it was reported that for every Englishman met on the streets there were four Spaniards "to the great discomfort of the English nation."[8] That was an understatement. The Spaniards were in real danger of being set upon and robbed each time they went out, especially after dark. One Spaniard wrote to express his point of view more potently:

> You may be certain that there are more sights to be seen here in England than are described in any book of chivalry: country houses, river-banks, woods, forests, delicious meadows, strong and beautiful castles, and everywhere fresh springs; for all these things abound here and make the country well worth a visit and most delightful, especially in summer-time. I might give you many more details of life here but to avoid tiring you, I will only say that we would rather be in Spain than see England or the sea, and we are all desiring to be off with such longing that we think of Flanders as Paradise. So now you may reflect on the way things are going in this realm.[9]

Renard feared that the continued enmity between Spanish and English could be dangerous to Philip, and urged him to leave England, taking the most "suspicious" Spanish characters with him. Philip decided that the best way to keep the peace was to reduce the number of his Spanish followers and send them away, retaining only a few of the most reliable.

Philip had not planned to leave England immediately after his marriage, though the intensified French offensive against the Emperor almost induced Charles to recall his son to his aid. However, Henry II's resources were also stretched. A lull in the fighting caused Charles to change his mind. "On the whole, therefore, we think you had better stay where you are and be with the Queen, my daughter, busying yourself with the government of England, settling affairs there and making yourself familiar with the people, which it is important you should do for present and future considerations."[10] Philip wrote shortly afterward: "For some days past I have been busying myself with affairs here and have made a good beginning."[11]

The Emperor did not spell it out, but he was hoping for several things to be accomplished by his son. First, Philip should be crowned King of England so that he would be in a position to direct affairs himself. As Mary's consort, officially he could only assist and advise the Queen privately. Unlike Jane Grey, who had refused to have her husband crowned, Mary was only too pleased to contemplate sharing her responsibilities or delegating them to someone else. But the idea met with strong opposition in other quarters. Mary's own Parliament, when considering the clauses of the marriage treaty, had provided against such a contingency. An Act of April 2, 1554, declared that "the Regal power of this Realm is in the Queen's Majesty as fully and absolutely as ever it was in any of her most noble Progenitors, Kings of this Realm,"[12] a measure intended to remove all danger of foreign intervention; Philip was to remain with the empty title of uncrowned King. Two of the Emperor's other aims for his son, however, were to meet with more success. On the spiritual side, Philip was to help return the erring sheep to the Papal fold; on the political front, he was to encourage England to support him actively in his war against France. The Emperor also hoped that Philip and Mary would produce an heir to help unite the Empire, which the Emperor feared might otherwise crumble at his death.

Renard, thinking his task completed once Philip and Mary were married, had asked to be allowed to return home. But the Emperor, considering Renard's experience in England and his knowledge of the vagaries of the various members of the Council too valuable to waste, ordered him to stay on as an adviser to Philip. Renard found his new role very different. The special relationship between him and the Queen had ended. Mary no longer needed to rely on him for comfort and advice. And his usefulness to Philip was diminished by the fact that they had no common language; he spoke no Spanish and Philip spoke no French. Renard had to be content to pass on his views in writing, hoping that his master would read, understand and take note. To add to Renard's feeling of redundancy, Philip had his own close friends from Spain to advise him, and they were no friends to the Fleming.

It is no wonder, therefore, that Renard was gloomy in his assessment of the state of affairs in England. The marriage had done nothing to bring together the disparate elements in the Council. The in-fighting continued. Gardiner and Paget were as inimical to each other as ever. There was still grave unrest in the country. The Protestants feared—with justification, as it turned out—the prospect of a return to Catholicism. And Elizabeth and Courtenay were still focal points for dissension, although they remained under guard. They did nothing that could bring them into conflict with the law, and openly proclaimed their loyalty and obedience to the monarchy and the church. But they were strongly suspected of secret connivance with the rebellious elements.

Just as Renard had formerly thought that the marriage would end at least some of the problems, he now believed that the birth of a royal prince might bring peace to the country. Elizabeth's demotion to second place in line for the throne would automatically decrease her importance. One of the Queen's physicians had told him it was probable that Mary was pregnant, he wrote to the Emperor in September. Whether it was true or not, he said he was going to spread the rumor in order to quiet the situation. Renard was not alone in this view. Two weeks later, when the news was confirmed by

*Simon Renard, Charles V's influential ambassador to the court of Mary I from 1553 to 1555. (Artist unknown, c. 1553.)* MANSELL COLLECTION, LONDON.

Mary, Gomez wrote "This pregnancy will put a stop to every difficulty."[13]

In November, Sir John Mason, English ambassador to the court of Charles V, said the Emperor was hoping for a man-child, but "be it man, be it woman, welcome shall it be; for by that shall we at last come to some certainty to whom God shall appoint, by succession, the government of our estate...."[14]

## 2. Back to Rome

Meanwhile Reginald Pole, the Papal Legate who had been waiting for permission to take up his post in England, was growing impatient. The Emperor had succeeded in having his arrival postponed until after the marriage in case his disapproval should help to prevent it. Four months later he was still in Europe. Another reason had been found to delay him. Serious efforts were certainly going to be made to establish the Catholic Church in England again, but there was one very definite obstacle which had to be overcome first. The Emperor was too much of a realist to believe that those who had benefited from the sharing out of the church lands after the dissolution of the monasteries would be willing to return them, even though many of those people would claim to be staunch Catholics. He suspected that this thought would not have occurred to Pole or, if it had, that his actions would not be influenced thereby. In order to achieve the desired result, it was therefore necessary to convince the Pope that an attempt to reclaim Church property would be unsuccessful and for him to instruct his Legate accordingly. With some difficulty this was done. In England, Philip reassured the Council on the same point. Council and Emperor then

*Reginald Pole, Cardinal and Papal legate. Archbishop of Canterbury from 1556 to 1558. One of Queen Mary's personal friends. (Artist unknown.) NATIONAL PORTRAIT GALLERY, LONDON.*

were in agreement that it was safe to allow Pole to return home.

After an absence of over twenty years, Reginald Pole landed in Dover on November 20, 1554. He was now 54 years old and, like so many others we have come across, in poor health. He was as wholeheartedly devoted to his Church as Mary was and, as Papal Legate and later Archbishop of Canterbury, he was in a strong position to uphold it. But his long absence had put him out of touch with the changed conditions in England. He was, perhaps even more than Mary, ignorant of the extent to which Protestantism had taken hold. He may have been mistaken in trying to reinstate a religion that was no longer held by the majority of the people and unconscious of the revolution that was taking place in their minds, but there can be no question about his good faith. According to the Venetian ambassador, Cardinal Pole was a man of unblemished nobility, "utterly undefiled by any sort of passion or worldly interest, as in what concerns his office he is not influenced either by the authority of Princes, nor by the ties of blood, of friendship, or of any other sort, being most strict with everybody and unparalleled."[15]

Ten days after his arrival, and the day after Mary's third Parliament had passed a "Petition for Reconciliation with Rome,"[16] Pole as Papal Legate gave his absolution for past errors. Roman Catholicism was once more the established religion. And Mary's unwanted title of Head of the Church in England and Ireland, taken by her father in 1531, had passed back into the hands of the Pope. All the Acts on religion passed by Henry VIII after the twentieth year of his reign (1529) were repealed, with the exception of those relating to the dissolution of the monasteries. Pole was not a willing accessory to this proviso, but there was nothing he could do except ask for a voluntary return of the properties—with the result that might have been expected.

The official return to Catholicism did not immediately bring a violent reaction. Rather, a feeling of euphoria percolated downward from the King and Queen to the staunch Catholics, through that large part of the population which did not feel deeply about religion one way or the other, to those Protestants who perhaps expected tolerance. There was always of course a hard core of Protestants who never ceased to be rebellious, but their less convinced followers for the moment were content to await events. The Queen's pregnancy also served to calm the monarchy-loving populace. Pole reported to the Pope: "Mary has spiritually regenerated England, before giving birth to that heir of whom there is very great hope."[17] In the same letter, he also made an illuminating remark on Philip's attitude to his wife: "Philip is the spouse of Mary, but treats her so deferentially as to appear her son."[18]

For the moment, things could not have been better for Mary. Her country was restored to the faith of her childhood. She had a charming, considerate husband whom she trusted to share her problems and to whom she could delegate some of her official duties. She believed herself to be pregnant and had been assured by her doctors that it was so. Following the custom of the time, she withdrew from public life in April to await the birth in the company of her ladies. She seemed quite content to allow Philip to deal with the Council. In her feeling of good will toward the world, she caused to be released from the Tower those who had been confined there for taking part in the Wyatt rebellion. Each man was given his freedom on his promise of good behavior and on payment of a fine.

Elizabeth and Courtenay shared in the amnesty. Several plans for Elizabeth's future had been considered with a view to minimizing her importance. Gardiner had wanted her illegitimacy to be reaffirmed; the idea of sending her to Brussels to the court of the Emperor's sister had been revived; marriage to a lesser foreign prince, which would have achieved the same result of taking her out of England, had been discussed. But Elizabeth was too astute to consent to the last and too popular with some members of the Council for the first two to be successful. She was released from Woodstock in May, some say as a result of Philip's intervention on her behalf. Sir Henry Bedingfield was instructed to bring her to Hampton Court, where she was kept waiting for two weeks before Mary consented to see her. Philip is said to have been curious enough to have visited her earlier, on which occasion Mary sent word to her to wear one of her richest gowns.[19] Mary was too innocent to suspect competition from her younger sister, and too trusting to fear that Philip might make comparisons (not to her own advantage) between the two. The Venetians, always ready to suspect fire at the slightest whiff of smoke, reported that Philip might already be considering her as his next wife if anything should happen to Mary.

Elizabeth resisted any attempts to make her show repentance, since to show repentance would have been equivalent to admitting guilt. When the sisters did confront each other she still maintained her innocence of any thought or act which could be construed as being against the Queen. Although Mary was still suspicious, she tried not to let her personal feelings affect her judgment. Elizabeth was freed from Bedingfield's guardianship. She was allowed to return to one of her own manors and spent the next few years in an apparently peaceful country existence, interspersed with occasional visits to Court. The fear of collusion between her and Courtenay, which he denied, was overcome by sending

Courtenay first to the Emperor in Brussels and then to voluntary exile in Italy. He did not live long to enjoy his freedom: he caught a chill and died in Padua the following year.

## 3. *Mary and the Martyrs*

The peaceful lull was short. Any hopes for religious toleration were soon shattered, for Parliament, as well as having restored the Catholic Church, had also revived the ancient laws of Richard II by which heresy was punished by burning. These laws, which had been considerably modified and eased by Henry VIII, again gave authority to the bishops for the arrest of anyone suspected of being a heretic.[20] The bishops could also advise the civil power whom to arrest and condemn and whom to hand over to them for trial.

The first Protestant martyr to suffer under the revived laws was John Rogers, a canon of St. Paul's. He was burned at the stake in London on February 3, 1555. Three more followed within a week. About 270 are reckoned to have suffered the same fate before the end of Mary's reign. Not all were serious Protestants quietly and bravely facing death for their faith, as More and Fisher had done for theirs. Some were young and rebellious, with no respect for authority; they taunted their judges, behaved badly in court and generally ridiculed their accusers, most of whom belonged to an older generation. Some were knaves, said the Venetian ambassador, with no other purpose than to disturb the peace and start an insurrection. Others were common criminals deserving punishment, but not the particular form of it which was inflicted on them. Nobody was safe from being denounced to the authorities by a private enemy or suspicious neighbor.

*Nicholas Ridley, Bishop of London. Protestant martyr, burned at the stake in 1555. (Artist unknown.)* NATIONAL PORTRAIT GALLERY, LONDON.

The most notable of those who can properly be called martyrs were Archbishop Cranmer and the Bishops Ridley and Latimer. From more or less comfortable lodgings in the Tower, they had been moved to Oxford the previous year in order to take part in a learned disputation about religion. They had afterward been condemned and kept in the common jail along with the ordinary criminals until the re-establishment of the Catholic Church had been completed. On October 16, Latimer and Ridley perished in the flames, meeting their death with fortitude. According to Foxe, Latimer encouraged his flagging companion at the end with the words which have since become famous: "Be of good comfort, Master Ridley, and play the man. We shall this day light such a candle by God's grace in England, as [I trust] shall never be put out."[21]

Cranmer was kept waiting several more months before his sentence was carried out, also at Oxford. He was first deprived of the office of archbishop and then handed over to the secular authority. Either through cowardice or confusion—perhaps a mixture of both—Cranmer recanted twice. But when the final moment came he denied his recantations. "At the moment when he was taken to the stake, he drew from his bosom the identical writing, throwing it, in the presence of the multitude, with his own hands into the flames.... And, finally, stretching forth his arm and right hand, he said, 'This, which has sinned, having signed the writing, must be the first to suffer punishment'; and thus did he place in the fire, and burned it himself."[22] After a life of mixed motives and mixed courage, but considerable achievement in the advancement of the Protestant faith, Cranmer bravely met his death on March 21, 1556. The Queen was said to have considered him unworthy of pardon. His martyr's death, however, encouraged her enemies to further efforts—not limited only to verse in favor of Elizabeth, such as the following:

When constant Cranmer lost his life
And held his hand into the fire;
When streams of tears for him were rife,
And yet did miss their just desire;
When Papish power put him to death,
We wished for our Elizabeth.[23]

Renard was disturbed when the burnings first started. On February 10, 1555, he wrote to the Emperor to acquaint him with the new situation in England. But the Queen, he said, was more popular than ever before. He concluded his letter with a remark which illustrated his own position very clearly: "I suppose that Señor Ruy Gomez will have informed your Majesty fully about this, and given you more authentic information than I can do, as I take no part in affairs."[24]

In spite of Renard's statement to the contrary, Mary's popularity had started to decline, though never during her lifetime was she hated as she was after her death. Innumerable books (such as John Knox's *Blast Against the Monstrous Regiment of Women*, pamphlets and ballads, some serious, some treasonable, some scurrilous, were circulated among the people. Formerly peaceful and loyal citizens found that their minds were being turned against their Queen, her husband, the Spaniards and the whole Catholic Church by the force of the polemics spread by the printed word. An unsuccessful attempt was made to halt this trend by the issue of a Royal Proclamation suppressing seditious books, including works by Luther, Zwingli, Calvin, Miles Coverdale, William Tyndale, Cranmer and the book commonly called *Hall's Chronicles*.

*Hugh Latimer, Bishop of Worcester. Protestant martyr burned at the stake in 1555. Said to have encouraged Ridley at the end with these words: "Be of good comfort, Master Ridley, and play the man. We shall this day light such a candle by God's grace in England as ... shall never be put out." (Artist unknown.) NATIONAL PORTRAIT GALLERY, LONDON.*

*John Foxe, author of* ACTS AND MONUMENTS, *commonly known as the* BOOK OF MARTYRS, *first published in England in 1563. (Artist unknown.)* NATIONAL PORTRAIT GALLERY, LONDON.

The most important of the publications was John Foxe's *Acts and Monuments*. Because of this book, in which were recorded unedited and unchecked versions of the lives of those he called indiscriminately the English Martyrs, Mary became known to succeeding generations as *Bloody Mary*. Foxe's book was an inaccurate, violently anti-Catholic work, though full of interesting and highly dramatic anecdotes. It was first published in Europe during Mary's lifetime, when Foxe had taken refuge abroad, and later in England a few years after Mary's death. It immediately achieved a tremendous popularity. It found a place in practically every church in the country, chained to the pulpit alongside the Bible. Some copies were still to be found in country churches as late as the nineteenth century. Its influence on public opinion was immeasurable, for it was taken as gospel truth. And popular assessments of Mary's character have been colored by it up to the present day. Only during the course of the last century was a serious attempt made to reappraise Mary—and Foxe. It was made not only by Catholics who hoped to recreate a more favorable image of Mary, but also by unprejudiced historians who wished to put her in her proper perspective.

It is hard to believe that Mary's character underwent such a sudden change, that she became as black, or as bloody, as she was afterward painted. Until 1555 she had always shown herself to be kind, thoughtful for others and over-ready to forgive. Both the Emperor and her Council had shown themselves to be more bloodthirsty. She had never of her own free will condemned even her recognized enemies to death; she would have forgiven Northumberland and Lady Jane Grey if her advisers had not persuaded her to the contrary. She tried never to let personal prejudice lead her into any action contrary to the law. Her treatment of Elizabeth was a case in point.

Contemporary descriptions of Mary up to this time had never failed to stress her piety and goodness. But, humane as Mary had always shown herself, she cannot be freed from some responsibility for the events of the last years of her life even though she did not instigate them. To say that at the beginning her mind was occupied with her private affairs—chiefly the preparations for the birth of her much desired child—and that she was therefore content to delegate her authority to Philip is not enough of an excuse. Even in her self-imposed segregation during her confinement, she cannot have been unconscious of what was happening in England. And the burnings continued when Philip went away.

In vain did Renard plead with Philip (and through him with Mary) to restrain the bishops: "I think your Majesty would be wise to show firmness and to tell the bishops that they are not to proceed to such lengths without having first consulted you and the Queen. . . Your Majesty might inform the bishops that there are other methods of chastising the obstinate, at this early stage."[25] Renard feared a revolt by both the nobility and the commoners who had accepted the Protestant form of religion—though the only word now used to describe them was "heretic." A few weeks later, he pressed the point further: "Haste in religious matters ought to be avoided. Cruel punishments are not the best way; moderation and kindness are required."[26] It was not only a humanitarian feeling which caused him to plead for restraint, but a pragmatic judgment: this was not the moment to punish the heretics in England. It would be better to work slowly and with caution until the old religion was again secure.

Mary showed however that she did not disapprove of the burnings. She went on record, in a memorandum which she wrote in her own hand and gave to

Pole, that she believed that preachers who deceived simple persons with false doctrine should be punished. They should be made to understand that they had not been condemned without just cause, and others thereby would know the truth and not be led to hold false opinions. "And above all I should wish that no one be burned in London save in the presence of some member of the Council; and that during such executions, both here and elsewhere, some good and pious sermons be preached."[27]

Mary's attitude could be explained by her regard for the law and her sincere religious beliefs. When the statutes on heresy made legal the punishment of heretics by burning, the Queen alone could not, and perhaps would not have wished to, prevent the law from taking its course, quite apart from her own feelings in the matter. She had not, in any case, the force of Henry VIII either to compel people to obey her or, if that had been her objective, to change the law.

More important was Mary's state of mind brought about by her almost fanatical piety. In her miserable and lonely youth Mary had found solace only in her prayers. Almost in self-defense, in her own stubborn way, she had become even more devout when oppressed during the reign of Edward VI. Long ago, she had feared for her father's soul: that he would fall from grace, not because of his treatment of her and her mother, but because of his denial of the Pope. Now she wanted the Protestant heretics, especially those who preached the new doctrine, to be saved from eternal damnation by the only means she had been taught— conversion or burning. At the same time, they would thus be prevented from spreading their heresies.

The story was told by later Protestant writers that Pole intended to have the corpse of Henry VIII removed from its resting place in Windsor Chapel and burned.[28] If this story is true, given the characters of both Mary and Pole, the late King is more likely to have been treated in this way in order to save his soul than to avenge past wrongs. If the two coffins discovered in the Henry VII Chapel in Westminster Abbey are, as thought, those of Henry VIII and Jane Seymour, the plan to burn the corpses cannot have been carried out.

The attitude of Reginald Pole toward the burning of the heretics is not clear. He was thought by Renard to be against it. He himself did not speak out. Before his return to England, however, he had stated his point of view in the letter he sent to Mary urging her to compel her subjects to honor God and to punish the disobedient by use of force if need be.* At least as staunch a Catholic as Mary, he believed that it was not the right moment, rather than that the punishment itself was wrong.

Philip did not positively support this treatment of the heretics in England, but basically he too did not believe it to be wrong. He was a Catholic. To him is attributed the saying: "Better not reign at all than reign over heretics."[29] And in Spain the *auto-da-fe* had been going on for years unchecked. There exists a rough draft in Philip's own hand from London in August where he says that members of Parliament "should take great care in their districts to punish offences against religion from now on,"[30] but he does not specify what kind of punishment. One of his attendant friars was said to have spoken out freely, saying that the bishops had not learned in Scripture to burn for conscience sake.[31] It is unlikely that he would have done so against his master's wishes. In any case, Philip cannot be held responsible for the continuation of the burnings for three and a half years. After the first six months, he was to be away from Eng-

*See page 136

land, except for one brief visit of four months in 1557, when he had other things on his mind.

It was Gardiner who first tried to have the ancient heresy laws reintroduced into England. Having failed to get Mary's second Parliament to agree, he was more successful with her third. Once the laws were reinstated, he worked actively against Cranmer and the Protestant bishops with the intention that they should be converted or punished. Paget told Renard of Gardiner's zeal, but Renard probably took the information with a grain of salt, knowing what enemies the two continued to be. Gardiner's enthusiasm for punishing the heretics lost its momentum as his own health failed. But Bonner, the Bishop of London who had succeeded Ridley on Mary's accession, then headed the bishops in their accusations. He too was a bloody man in Foxe's eyes, but he was not alone nor indeed as bad as he was painted. He and the other bishops were inspired originally by religious beliefs but then were carried away on the wave of a movement that got out of control.

Not all heretics were rebels, nor all rebels heretics. Renard, and also Mary, thought when the disturbers of the peace became more numerous, that it would be better to distinguish between the two. The punishment for a rebel was to cut off his head, not to burn him. The bishops were not prepared to make distinctions and proceeded as before without consulting Mary.

Thus it can be seen that the first responsibility for the conflagrations* lay with Gardiner. This responsibility he shared with the Members of Parliament who voted to allow the heresy laws to be revived and with the bishops, headed by Bonner, who carried them out. Mary, Philip and Pole cannot be exonerated, however, as they did nothing by word or deed to try to halt the

*It is interesting to note that the date given by the *Oxford English Dictionary* for the first known use of the word is 1555.

*Stephen Gardiner, Bishop of Winchester. As Lord Chancellor during Mary's reign was in favor of burning the Protestants. Died 1555. (Artist unknown.) MASTER AND FELLOWS OF TRINITY COLLEGE, CAMBRIDGE.*

burnings. To a lesser degree, the English people who attended the burnings and who denounced to the authorities those neighbors whom they suspected or had a grudge against can also be held accountable.

It is, however, important not to judge the sixteenth century by the standards of the twentieth. The normal death rate at all age levels was high. Families must have faced their losses with some equanimity, or they would have been perpetually in a state of grief. Belief in an after-life encouraged both those who had to leave this earth and those who were left behind. Violent death too was not unusual. Punishments were severe for many offenses that today would be considered minor ones. Burning at the stake was the accepted punishment for heretics, as hanging or the electric chair were until recently the accepted punishment for murderers in our generation.

Mary was not moved by personal considerations. She did not send her enemies to their death as her father had done and as her sister was to do later. She spared Elizabeth when pressed to get rid of her, but Elizabeth was not to spare Mary, Queen of Scots. Finally, it should be remembered that less than three hundred died in Mary's reign compared with thousands in the reign of Henry VIII. Even so, the end of her reign was certainly bloody compared with the beginning, though she does not deserve the epithet. Her bigotry destroyed her reputation for clemency.

## 4. The Expected Child

Everything had been made ready at Hampton Court for the royal child expected in early June. The announcements only needed to have the blank spaces filled in with the name of the child and the date of birth.

But as the weeks went by, there began to be doubts as to whether Mary was really pregnant. First it was said that a mistake had been made in the reckoning. (Gomez reported on June 8 that the calculation was out by two months.) Eventually Mary's doctors realized their diagnosis had been wrong, but Mary did not want to believe them. She was big and she was sure she had felt the child move within her. Her ladies kept up the pretense out of a mistaken sense of kindness.

Even allowing for the primitive state of the medical profession, it is surprising that her physicians continued to be deceived by her condition until the end. Mary had led so sheltered an existence herself that she was possibly ignorant of the whole cycle of childbearing except for such information as she had been given by her ladies. We do not know the clinical details but we do know that Mary had never had regular periods. Amenorrhea can lead to edema of the body and the swelling could give the appearance of pregnancy. If, in addition, Mary so passionately desired a child, it would not have been difficult for her to imagine she had all the symptoms her ladies had described. False pregnancies are not uncommon.

Mary's state of mind when she at last realized the truth scarcely bears to be thought about.* To add to her distress, she knew that Philip was preparing to leave for Brussels to visit his father, who, it was rumored, wanted to abdicate. She knew too that Philip's disappointment would be great and that, through no fault of her own, she had failed the Emperor whose hopes for a man-child to inherit and unite England and the Netherlands were not to be fulfilled.

Mary had also to summon up her courage to face the world again, for since April she had rarely left her

---

*The clothes she had prepared for her expected child were kept and can still be seen at Hever Castle.

own apartments in the palace. And part of the outside world was being far from kind. Satirical verses and lampoons on her condition were circulated in London, though perhaps they never reached her sight—and there was also a rumor that she had died. To add to her troubles, the English summer was the worst in living memory, with the result that the harvest was ruined and the people discontented. In August, Mary consented to leave Hampton Court, which was said to be in need of cleaning after having been continuously inhabited for four months. The many ladies who had come from all over England to be present at the birth were sent home again, "and by degrees her Majesty has resumed the audiences, and replaced other matters in their former ancient state,"[32] reported the Venetian ambassador, Michiel. (During the next few years, the Venetian dispatches give the most insight into events. Renard's importance had already diminished and his reports had become fewer even before he left the country for France.)

A few weeks later, after the palace had been put in order, Mary and Philip returned to Hampton Court, "And now the Queen shows herself and converses with everybody as usual, her health being so good, as perhaps never to have been better, to the universal surprise of all who see her, but of delivery or pregnancy small signs are visible externally and no one talks or thinks of them any longer."[33] But Philip was preparing to leave and felt it necessary to dissemble: "It is said he will leave in eight or ten days, postwise, leaving the greater part of his household for the sake of convincing the Queen by as many signs as he can, that he purposes returning speedily; though on the contrary, it is said more than ever, that he will go to Spain, and remove his household and all the others by degrees."[34]

Before Philip left, he and Mary rode through the streets of London accompanied by the Papal Legate, the

*The Royal Palace at Greenwich. (From an engraving by Brasire, pub-
lished by the Society of Antiquaries, 1767.) Folger Shakespeare Library,
Washington, D.C.*

ambassadors, the Lord Mayor and all the usual digni-
taries. Such is the fickleness of crowds that the procession received a tremendous ovation, all the greater
"as the London populace were convinced that the
Queen was dead." Philip said goodbye to Mary at
Greenwich. Elizabeth too was present. He kissed all the
ladies as he had been taught in England, and the Spaniards kissed Mary's hand. Mary then watched from one
of the windows of the palace as Philip went past on his
barge on his way down the river to the coast. He waved
his bonnet from the distance and Mary waited until he
was out of sight.

Mary, who in public had concealed her feelings
of sorrow at her husband's departure and her humilia-

tion and grief over the fiasco of her pregnancy, in private could not control her tears. "As may be imagined with regard to a person extraordinarily in love, the Queen remains disconsolate, though she conceals it as much as she can, and from what I hear mourns the more when alone and supposing herself invisible to any of her attendants."[35] While Philip waited for favorable weather to sail from Dover to Calais, he maintained his attitude of devotion to Mary. They exchanged notes until, on September 4, 1555, he left the coast of England behind him.

*Mary I*

# CHAPTER VII

# THE QUEEN ALONE

## 1. *London and Brussels*

Philip had no intention of returning quickly to England, although he had implied the contrary. And his departure was only delayed because he was waiting for money. "I do not mean to delay further for any other reason than this. Do your best to see that nothing detains me for much time has gone past, far more than was needed,"[1] he had written in a note before he left. It was not only that he was dissatisfied with his English life, but he knew that important events about to take place in Brussels would keep him busy. The fleet which had taken him across the Channel was dismissed after he had disembarked at Calais. Mary was upset at the news. She would not contemplate the thought that Philip had left her for any length of time although others freely discussed the probability. She immediately had the ships reassembled and made ready to bring back her husband to England the moment he was ready. As it turned out, the ships waited for six months before Mary herself decided to disband them.

For over a year Philip had successfully impressed the Queen, the Court and the Council, and, more surprisingly, his father with his politeness and willingness to adapt to English ways. The all-knowing Venetian ambassador could not say other than that Philip was the most loving and tender of husbands. Some said he was unfaithful, but the two statements were not necessarily contradictory. Mary knew of his infidelities, but still believed in his love for her. "If she does not hold the King chaste, I at least know that she says she believes him free from love for any other woman,"[2] wrote Michiel. Like her mother, she probably accepted such behavior as part of the *mores* of the day.

Philip's scrupulous observance of the articles of the marriage treaty, his tact, and his masterly understanding of government had obtained him certain concessions. It had been agreed that the minutes of the Council should be written in Spanish or Latin and, even though Parliament had refused to crown Philip as King, they had been willing for him to become Regent during the minority of the child if Mary had died. The position of authority with the Council which he had achieved illustrated the truth of Renard's diagnosis: "The Council's authority is impaired by the natural fickleness and ambition of the English, this kingdom being a popular* one, in which nobility has no other authority than that entrusted to it by the King. . . There is more external show than inner stability, and therefore authority is needed in order to impose a competent administration."[3]

Philip had done what he could to safeguard Mary's position while he was away. He probably shared Gomez's opinion of the Queen: "The Queen is a good soul, but not as able as we were led to suppose—I mean

*populaire in the original French text, i.e., supported by the people

as a stateswoman."[4] Philip knew that she needed some trusted friend on whom she could depend for advice, and did not have to look further than Cardinal Pole, for whom he also had a high regard. As the old Council had been too large and unwieldy, a new Council was formed consisting of only nine members.* Philip left the government of the country in their charge but asked Pole to act as Mary's chief adviser.

Pole was given lodgings in Greenwich Palace, where Mary had chosen to stay during her husband's absence. Philip could not have done better for Mary's comfort than to leave her with her old friend, but whether Pole's guidance was equally good for the country is a different matter. His religious fervor was strong, but his ability as a statesman poor. He was more likely to encourage Mary in her intolerance, especially now that Renard's restraining influence had been removed. Renard had left England about the same time as Philip and Mary had shown her appreciation of his services in a letter to the Emperor.** "I assure you, Sire, that he was here with me through very dangerous times, and that he showed himself during the marriage negotiations to be a most indispensable minister, inspired by the greatest desire to serve us and the greatest zeal for my affairs."[5]

The authority which Mary had once so eagerly looked forward to sharing with Philip was now, theoretically, once more hers alone. But she was still incapable of making up her mind without advice. Although she grew to depend more and more upon Pole, she also

---

*The Cardinal (Pole), the Chancellor (Gardiner), the Treasurer (William Powlett), the Earls of Arundel and Pembroke, the Bishop of Ely (Thirlby), Lords Paget, Rochester and Petre (Secretary).

**There had been no need for an ambassador from the Emperor as long as Philip was in England. Nobody was appointed in Renard's place, though Figueroa (known as the Regent) stayed behind with no official position aided by the Count of Feria.

wrote constantly to Philip to seek his counsel. Pole too kept Philip informed about affairs in England and about Mary's welfare: "The Queen passes the forenoon in prayer after the manner of Mary and in the afternoon admirably personates Martha, by transacting business."[6] Three weeks later he wrote that such was the Queen's assiduity in the despatch of business that she passed the greater part of the day in this occupation and the night in writing to Philip, to the injury of her health.[7]

Mary realized that she could not stay in Greenwich indefinitely praying for Philip to return to relieve her of her heavy responsibilities. There were official duties which could not be postponed or performed outside London. Mary moved therefore to St. James's Palace. On October 21, she opened Parliament with all the customary pageantry. Cardinal Pole accompanied her as Philip was not back. Gardiner, whose health was failing fast, made what was to be his last appearance as Chancellor. In spite of his weakness, he managed with all his old skill to achieve his objective—to get promises for more money to fill the empty coffers of the Crown. Just over three weeks later, on November 12, he died. Mary had lost a good servant. His advice had not always been acceptable and he had made mistakes of judgment, but his loyalty to her as Queen was never suspect. He knew the temper of the Council better than Pole ever would. And Gardiner had also been a very good Chancellor in difficult times. The same cannot be said of the man who succeeded him, Nicholas Heath, Bishop of Worcester.

Philip did not lose touch with events in England. Besides hearing from Mary and Pole, he received the Council's minutes which he scrutinized carefully, annotated, and returned. He had favored Paget for Chancellor, but Mary, perhaps partly under Pole's influence, felt that the post should go to a churchman and, rather surprisingly, went against Philip's advice. Paget's position was nevertheless strengthened by the death of his enemy. His failure to become Chancellor was to some extent compensated by his being made Lord Privy Seal. Renard had never trusted Paget, although he had been so helpful in drawing up the marriage treaty, and believed him to be secretly plotting against the Queen and supporting Elizabeth. Paget in fact was insuring his own future by service to both. Mary also had no confidence in him and looked upon the rest of the Council with the same suspicion she had always had of them. She had to rely on them but did so unwillingly. Pole was her only trusted support in the King's absence.

Philip arrived in Brussels in mid-September. Four days later the Emperor openly expressed the thought that was in both their minds, the thought which Mary did not want to accept: "There is no longer any hope of her being with child."[8] Lack of an heir did not change their immediate plans for uniting England and the Netherlands, but the future government of the Empire had to be rethought. There was also the problem of what would happen in England on Mary's death. Bearing this in mind, Philip always encouraged Mary to be lenient toward her sister who was still next in line for the throne.

Philip's behavior underwent a marked change when he was back among friends. He no longer had to disguise his feelings: his disappointment at not being crowned, his frustration when he knew there would be no heir, his irritation about the treatment the Spaniards received in England, his anger at the way he was lampooned in the popular pamphlets and ballads. Now he could relax, which he did to such effect that he drew a reproof from his father for his frivolous ways. And Mary's messengers, who had brought Philip her letters

*Philip II (Artist unknown.)* NATIONAL MARITIME MUSEUM, LONDON.

and tokens of love, dared not report back to her how he was enjoying himself.[9]

Mary fretted when a week went by without a letter from Philip. But his personal letters became less frequent and apparently less loving. The Venetian ambassador in Brussels reported that Philip had written to Mary that he would have liked to gratify her wish for his return but he could not adapt himself to reside in England in a form unbecoming his dignity. What he had been too polite to say, he was not afraid to write. Later Philip sent a message that he would be returning soon after Christmas. But instead of coming back, he ordered some of his household in England to Brussels and some to Spain. Mary was filled with foreboding, but the English people rejoiced to see the Spaniards leave and speeded them on their way with "a variety of foul language."[10] Philip also made no special effort to get on well with the English in Brussels. He was not afraid to let them know that he resented that the crown was withheld. He still needed that authority in order to demand English support in his struggle with France. Much as Mary would have liked to please him, she had to confess herself unable to press Parliament on these points for fear of starting another rebellion.

The chief reason for Philip's departure from England was indeed the one that had already been rumored. The Emperor wished to abdicate in favor of his son. He had decided to carry out this decision after hearing of the death of his mother Juana who nominally shared the government of Spain with him. She had died on April 11 in Tordesillas. The news of her death had reached England about the time Mary went into seclusion at Hampton Court. Philip had expressed what he called "a reasonable regret." Gomez had written rather sourly: "The mourning costs us a fortune; all the English pensioners* have come along demanding black suits and behaving as if their honor would be tarnished if they did not obtain them. So we have put more folk into mourning in this Kingdom than have ever been seen here, or ever will be."[11]

The Emperor was not told till June, though he said that he had heard his mother's voice calling him when she died. He too was prone to the melancholy which had afflicted her. At the age of fifty-five, he was tired and in pain all the time. He was anxious therefore to retire to Yuste in Spain where he was building a house near a monastery. Here he hoped to spend his last days in peace playing with the hundred clocks which had become his chief amusement. He would also be free from all responsibility toward Mary. That function he had delegated to his son and Mary had willingly accepted the substitute. During his last months in Brussels the only personal letters he received from Mary always contained a plea to send Philip back to her or to complain that the Emperor had not carried out his promise to do so.

> I implore your Majesty most humbly, for the love of God, to do all that is possible to permit it. I see every day that the end of one negotiation is the beginning of another. I beg your Majesty to forgive my boldness, and to remember the unspeakable sadness I experience because of the absence of the King, which emboldens me thus to write to you, who have always shown me a more than paternal affection.[12]

About the time Mary was opening Parliament in London, preparations were going ahead in Brussels for the great ceremony in which Philip would take over from his father. First, on October 22, Philip was made

*i.e., those receiving pensions from the Emperor and Philip

Grand Master of the Golden Fleece, one of the highest orders of Knighthood. Three days later Charles handed over the sovereignty of Burgundy and the Low Countries to his son. On January 16, 1556, he ceded his Spanish territories. The Emperor's brother Ferdinand was to inherit Austria and the German states over which he already ruled in practice. Only the now empty title of Emperor Charles kept for himself.

Philip, before he was thirty years of age, had become King of Spain, Naples and Sicily and Duke of Milan; he ruled over Burgundy and the Low Countries; he had possessions in Africa; he owned the Philippines (named after him) and the Spice Islands in the Pacific; Mexico, Peru and parts of the West Indies were his. But it still rankled him that he was uncrowned in England. When he sent a messenger to Mary to tell her the news of his accession, he was perhaps not only rejoicing in his newly gained power, but also underlining how much she had gained from the marriage and how little he had. (It is strange therefore that most of the diplomatic letters of the day refer to Philip as the King of England, not by any of his other titles.) Philip said again that he would shortly be returning to her. Whether he meant it or not, Mary believed him. She sent the fleet to Dover to be ready to escort him, but both she and the fleet waited in vain.

Another development helped to delay Philip's return. The Emperor and his two widowed sisters, Mary, Queen of Hungary, and Eleanor, who had been married to Francis I, delayed their departure to Spain for another eight months. For some time Charles V had been trying to come to terms with Henry II. He did not wish to bequeath the struggle with France to his son, nor the drain on the exchequer which it involved. Renard, when he left England, had been sent to France to negotiate a treaty, and as a result a five-year truce was signed on

February 5, 1556. Philip no longer had need to return to England in order to gain support for his war.

## 2. The "Dudley" Rebellion

In England a more than usually menacing situation developed around Mary. At the beginning of 1556, a far-reaching plot was gradually uncovered, the whole story of which never became clear.[13] The French were thought to have been the chief instigators, supported by a large number of English dissentients, though the nominal leader was Sir Henry Dudley, a relative of Jane Grey's husband and the Duke of Northumberland. It was said that if the plot had been successful Courtenay and Elizabeth would have been put on the throne, and Mary together with various unnamed people including several foreigners would have been murdered.

In March, a comet with a fiery tail had been visible in London for several days before Cranmer was to be burned alive. A gang of rogues played upon the superstitious nature of the people by crying that the Day of Judgment was at hand when everything would be consumed in the flames. To simulate the truth of their prophecy they started several fires in different parts of the city. They were arrested, and it turned out that there were to have been many more fires under cover of which several people would have been murdered and the Tower of London attacked and robbed of its store of coins and bullion. "Had it [the plot] been carried into effect as arranged, it would doubtless, as generally believed, considering the ill-will the majority of the population have on account of religion, besides their innate love of change and innovation, have placed the Queen and the whole Kingdom in great trouble, as it was of

*Sir William Paget, made Lord Privy Seal by Mary in 1556.*
*(Attributed to Master of the Statthalterin Madonna)*
NATIONAL PORTRAIT GALLERY, LONDON.

greater circuit and extent than had been at first supposed."[14] But one conspirator had second thoughts. He
informed Cardinal Pole and so the rebellion was suppressed before it had properly begun.

Mary was frightened. She no longer appeared in
public and she would not allow Pole to leave her to go
to Canterbury to receive Cranmer's archbishopric. (Instead, he was consecrated at Greenwich in the church
where Mary had been christened.) More than ever Mary
longed for Philip to be with her and was hurt that he still
showed no signs of joining her. The Venetian ambassador in Brussels reported that it was being said there
that "the Queen is beyond measure exasperated by what
she considers this well-nigh contemptuous treatment received from her consort."[15]

Paget, as the member of the Council most likely
to be acceptable to Philip, was sent to Brussels in April
ostensibly, to congratulate the Emperor and Philip on
their truce with France. It was no secret however that
his real aim was not only to encourage Philip to return
but also to find out whether there was some hidden
motive for his delay. It became clear to Paget during his
stay that the Emperor, not yet having left for Spain,
did not wish Philip to return to England as his own
departure would thereby be harder to justify and that
Philip himself had no intention of going back to England
until he was absolutely sure that he would be crowned
King. Paget tried every ruse he knew to make Philip
believe that his wish could easily be fulfilled once he
was again in London and found an unexpected ally in the
Queen of Hungary. She would have welcomed her
nephew's departure, as she would then have remained
Regent of the Netherlands instead of having to accompany Charles to Spain, for she had resigned rather than
work under Philip. "However much she may love King
Philip ... she need not stress how hard it would be for

her, having served the Emperor for twenty-five years, to start learning her ABC again now that she is past fifty. There is much youth about, with whose ways she is not in sympathy. Many people are corrupt, and the upright are few,"[16] she was reported to have written to the Emperor. Philip however did not believe Paget and, having heard that he himself was to have been one of the victims of the plot in England was even more determined not to return.

Paget, his mission unaccomplished, came home in May to find that new ramifications of the conspiracy were still being discovered and that the situation was far more serious than had at first been thought. Dudley and several of his fellow plotters had been in France when the rebellion broke out—prematurely as it turned out and had taken refuge at the court of Henry II. An English delegation was then sent to the French King to complain that he was harboring English rebels. Henry disclaimed all responsibility and went so far as to say that he would welcome any Englishman who took refuge in France. De Noailles, however, was so openly involved that he asked to be recalled "to avoid dishonor." In reality he feared that the conspirators who had been arrested might compromise him while under examination and that his diplomatic immunity might not protect him. This wish was granted and he was replaced by his brother.

Elizabeth was clearly implicated, though she was clever enough to leave no proof. Mary believed her to have been a willing accomplice and was angry. She would have liked to see the source of so much scandal and disturbance removed to Brussels, but the opposition to such a plan would have been great, for Elizabeth had a strong following both in the Council and in the country. The moves which were made against her were more diplomatic and probably instigated by Philip, who could at a distance take a more objective view of the situation. Mary had kept him fully informed of events as they occurred and his advice was sent to her by return. Philip was also not unaware that he himself might at some time be in need of help from those who supported Elizabeth. He still advocated that she should marry the Duke of Savoy, who owed allegiance to him and whom he thought he could control. But Elizabeth successfully evaded that issue when it was suggested to her by bursting into tears in front of Mary. Mary's own eyes also filled with tears and she did not press the point. Elizabeth was not called to account, but her governess Mrs. Ashley and several members of her household were arrested and sent to the Tower. Loyal Catholics were substituted for her Protestant attendants and her every move was watched. Sir Thomas Pope, "a rich and grave gentleman," unwillingly accepted the post of Governor of her house. She was not a prisoner and was received by Mary with as sweet words as she gave, but nevertheless she knew she was surrounded by spies. Mary had reproduced for her sister, though with much more kindness, the situation she herself had been made to undergo in an earlier day.

About forty conspirators were arrested, including some who had been lately freed from the Tower by Mary in spite of advice to the contrary. In the course of the next few weeks, a few of them were hanged, drawn and quartered and their dismembered bodies placed on the city gates as a warning to others. In the atmosphere of hysteria resulting from the plot, the burning of the heretics also was intensified. "They have continued during the present week ... to burn male and also female heretics, all of whom, so far from evincing fear of the flames, seek them voluntarily, accusing themselves ... proof that the thing has taken root, not only with the young but with their elders,"[17] reported Michiel. But in spite of the horrible deaths inflicted in the excitement of the moment on the first of those condemned as traitors, many more of the guilty were less severely punished and some were pardoned on payment of a fine. Dr. Cheke, Edward VI's former tutor, was allowed to go free after admitting his sins and embracing the Catholic Church.

The plot failed, as the earlier Wyatt rebellion had failed, because the conspirators were not well coordinated and because one of them turned informer. But this plot was far more dangerous and embraced far more people. There was moreover another important difference: Mary herself played no important role in rallying her people and showed no signs of courage. It was left to Pole to preach a sermon of comfort and cheer.

To make matters worse in the country, the summer of 1556 was as hot and dry as the previous summer had been cold and wet. Again there was a prospect of a poor harvest and the further unrest and discontent that would bring. In August Mary was ill—partly because of the heat, partly because of her state of mind. She lost weight and could not sleep. She left the government of the kingdom to Pole and retired to Croydon, at that time still in the country.

Mary's clemency was sorely tried when she saw how it had been turned against her. She was not able to cope with the situation and decided to postpone all decisions till Philip returned . . . "and the execution of those condemned to death is deferred from what I hear, until her return, perhaps in order that the King being then here may, with his usual clemency, obtain their entire release, so as to gain for himself so much the more favor and popularity."[18]

Mary sought solace in her religion and in religious practices. A Venetian in London described the Holy Week ceremony in which she took a leading part.[19] On Maundy Thursday, accompanied by Pole and her ladies, she washed the feet of forty-one poor women, "such being the number of the years of the most serene Queen," The women were seated on benches in a large hall with their right feet on stools. The Queen and her ladies wore long linen aprons and round their necks hung long towels. "One of the menials of the Court, having washed the right foot of each of these poor persons" the Under Almoner and the Grand Almoner then performed the same function. The Queen proceeded to wash the right foot of each woman there and then "kissed the foot so fervently that it seemed as if she were embracing something very precious." She then gave each of them enough food for four persons, wine, cloth to make clothing, shoes and stockings, and a leather purse containing forty-one pennies. She also gave them all the towels and aprons she and her ladies had used. Finally, she changed her dress and gave it to the poorest woman present—"this gown was of the finest purple cloth, lined with marten's fur and with sleeves so long and wide that they reached the ground." The next day she blessed the scrofulous. For three women and one man she pressed with her fingers in the form of a cross "on the spot where the sore was, with such compassion and devotion as to be a marvel."

In September, much improved in health, Mary returned to London. It pleased her to see that some abbeys were being repeopled with monks even though the majority of them remained empty and in ruins. But the general situation in England she still found very distressing. Mary wrote to the Emperor from her heart: "I wish to beg your Majesty's pardon for my boldness in writing to you at this time, and humbly to implore you, as you have always been pleased to act as a true father to me and my Kingdom, to consider the miserable plight into which this country has now fallen. I have written to the King, my husband, in detail on the subject, and I assure your Majesty that I am not moved by my personal desire for his presence, although I confess I do unspeakably long to have him here, but by my care for this Kingdom. Unless he comes to remedy matters, not I only but also wiser persons than I fear that great danger will ensue for lack of a firm hand, and indeed we see it before our eyes."[20] It is unlikely however that the Emperor ever received this letter, as about this time he at last left Brussels for Spain.

The following month Mary was overjoyed to hear that the King's pages, stables and armory had arrived at Dover, together with some shopkeepers who normally followed the Court. This was surely a sign that Philip would soon be on his way. But again Mary was to be disappointed, though this time she knew the reason for his nonappearance. Philip was at war with the Pope.

There was a great deal of interchange of messengers between London and Brussels, though the reason was kept secret. The return journey from London to Brussels took one messenger only five days with a stay in Brussels of one and a half days. Michiel noted the flurry of activity and suspected something of gravity and importance was being discussed but could only guess what it was: some fresh conspiracy with the French behind it had been discovered; some design of the French on fortresses either in England or across the Channel had come to light; or a request from the King to the Queen that, should the truce be broken, England would come to his aid. Michiel's sources were good and probably a mixture of all three was involved.

But Christmas was near and Mary decided to keep the festivities in Greenwich. The hot summer had been succeeded by a freezing winter. Mary was not able to travel down the river in her barge because of the ice. She crossed the Thames to Lambeth where she dined with Pole in his palace, meeting for the first time and at her own request Monsignor Priuli, Pole's lifelong friend who had followed him to London. Then she got into her litter and continued the journey by land to spend a lonely Christmas with no prospect of Philip's imminent return.

## 3. War

In the fall of 1556 the Catholic King Philip, one of whose chief aims had been to return England to the papal fold, found himself provoked into war with the Pope. The Catholic King Henry II, while suppressing his own Protestants in France, was at the same time supporting the English Protestant rebels. This seemingly paradoxical situation illustrates the interming ling of religious and political factors, with the latter generally more decisive.

The previous year, a new Pope, the eighty-year-old Paul IV, had been elected in a somewhat irregular way. A Neapolitan by birth, he hated Spaniards in general because of their sovereignty over Naples, and Philip in particular because Philip had opposed his nomination as Pope and had suggested Reginald Pole as an alternative. Paul IV had not much difficulty in persuading the French to break their newly made truce with Philip in order to help him expel the Spaniards. As a reward, he promised to give Naples to the French King's son. Philip now had two enemies to face, two fronts on which to fight and a perpetual shortage of money with which to pay his men. He was however still a formidable foe for the Pope to take on. His temporal authority equalled that of the Pope in spiritual matters.[21] His command of material resources was greater in spite of his impecunious state. His territories and his soldiers were conveniently close to Rome compared with those of the French King; the Duke of Alva, who led Philip's troops, was within a year able to march triumphantly through the streets of the Holy City.

As long as the war lasted Mary was troubled, her loyalties yet once more divided. She did not appreciate the political shadings of the conflict or the territorial aspects which mattered more to Paul and Philip than religious unanimity. But she understood that Philip now had a legitimate excuse to postpone his arrival in England. She knew too that because he was at war with the Pope that did not mean that the English Protestants would rally to his side. Their hatred of the Spaniards was as great as their hatred of the Pope. England remained neutral. Mary wrote many letters to Paul IV pleading with him to come to terms with Philip, "King of England, husband of a most Catholic Queen," and she did all she could to persuade Philip to make peace. Even so, the Pope was dissatisfied with her efforts, believing that she had helped Philip with money—which was indeed true.

Above all else Philip needed money, and he had already borrowed so much that he could now only borrow at extremely high rates of interest. He decided that he must make more serious efforts to persuade England to help him. If active participation was ruled out by the articles of the wedding treaty, he could at least legitimately ask for some troops and money for the defense of the Netherlands. For this reason and this reason alone he was willing to postpone his demand for the Crown and to return to England. He knew Mary was not capable of swinging opinion in his favor but he believed that he himself still had enough authority to persuade the Council. The French said, however, that Mary had bribed him to return by offering him her support in the war. In February 1557 he sent Gomez to inform Mary that he was shortly to join her and to tell Paget what his real intentions were. On March 24, Philip arrived in London. Mary was overjoyed to see him, ready to forget her former sorrow and exasperation in the pleasure of having him by her side again, willing to take control of the situation. Renard accompanied Philip on his visit to England, having been expelled from France earlier in the year when the truce came to nothing. But he wrote no reports or, if he did, none have come down to us. Michiel was recalled by the Venetians at the end of 1556 and left early the following year. He was then sent as their ambassador to Paris. He was replaced by Michiel Surian whose reports were rather more pedestrian than were those of his predecessor.

Philip's arrival, however, created a difficult situation for Cardinal Pole. As the Pope's Legate in England he could not be received officially by the King, as the King was at war with the Pope. He overcame this problem by retiring from public life to his See at Canterbury after first visiting the King in his private capacity. He informed the Pope of what he had done (as did the French who naturally put the worst construction on his actions and pretended to be shocked). In any case the Pope had no love for the Cardinal, his former rival. In April he deprived Pole of his power as Legate in England and summoned him back to Rome. In June he replaced him with the eighty-year-old Friar Peto who was far too old and feeble to be of much help to Mary. Peto himself was unwilling to undertake the duties and tried to refuse. He shortly afterward resolved his own problem by dying.

Pole and his many friends were taken aback by the announcement of his recall. Mary urged the Pope to reconsider for, she said, England would relapse into Protestantism without a powerful Papal representative.

But Pole also had enemies. According to Michiel, "as he [Pole] is beloved and revered by the King and Queen, and universally, so is he in secret envied and hated by some of those who rule, because they are no longer able to advance themselves by authority and favor as they were used to do formerly, having to submit and refer everything to him..."[22] The irascible old Pope let it be known that Pole was required in Rome to answer a charge of heresy before the Inquisition. No one has ever believed the devout and faithful Pole to have been guilty of such a charge. On behalf of her trusted old friend and relative, the equally devout Mary was even prepared to deny the authority of the Pope she had revered all her life by having the couriers from Rome intercepted so that the Papal demands should not reach her or Pole.

The question of Pole's return to Rome remained unanswered as long as Philip's troops were fighting in Italy. Afterward it was left in abeyance until Pole's death brought the dispute to an end. Meanwhile, Pole stayed on as Archbishop of Canterbury. Deprived of the authority that had been invested in him by the Pope, he was able to accede to the request of the King and Queen to return to the Council, where his presence had been missed.

Philip did not find it as easy as he had expected to raise money and men in England. "I hope affairs here will go well," he wrote, "although I have found there has been a little more hardening than I had expected."[23] Although poverty was by no means uncommon among the rulers of Europe, Mary's poverty was obvious enough to be reported and commented on by foreign ambassadors. In spite of her lack of money, she had dutifully renounced any Crown income which Henry VIII and Edward VI had taken from the Church and had given it to Pole to use for ecclesiastical and educational purposes. She was therefore even poorer than before. She had tried to raise money by a new tax on the people, "taking from each according to his means," in order to cover the cost of quelling the insurrection. Parliament was ever suspicious that demands for money were in the end destined for Philip's use, so that to raise money for him openly was well-nigh impossible. Mary borrowed wherever she could, Thomas Gresham being her chief agent for this purpose in Europe. She sold off Crown property, the whole of the money realized going immediately to Philip, "as the Queen thinks solely of giving his Majesty every possible assistance, nor does she attend to anything else."[24]

But Fate, in the form of France herself, played into Philip's hands. French support of the English rebels became so blatant that war with France was no longer to be considered as Philip's war. Mary herself had always resented the continual involvement of the French in conspiracies against her and their support of Elizabeth. French participation in the Dudley plot had also stirred up some popular feeling. Further events now served to increase the general mistrust and to drive the English into war with France of their own accord.

Thomas Stafford, grandson of the late Duke of Buckingham, had been deeply involved in the Dudley conspiracy. He had since been living in France, still full of ideas for bringing Mary down and greatly improving his own position. With the aid of Henry II he hatched a daring plot. In April 1557 he sailed across the North Sea with some forty companions in two armed French ships. He landed in Yorkshire and easily captured Scarborough Castle which, as it was not a very important fortification, was not well guarded. The ships sailed on to Scotland with French soldiers intended as reinforcements for their Scottish allies. Stafford expected the northern counties to rally immediately to his side. But he had mistaken the temper of their people. Many of them were Catholics and loyal to the Queen—Mary had, after all, once considered making her headquarters in York in order to be among friends. An army was sent against the rebels and Stafford capitulated at once. His Yorkshire supporters were hanged on the spot. He was brought to London and beheaded. Some twenty-five of the men who had come from France with him were also captured and they were hanged. It was said that he had expected support from Elizabeth, whom he had intended to marry so that they could ascend the throne together. Again Elizabeth was suspect.

Still more French troops were sent to Scotland, and it was suspected that they were destined for aggressive action on the English-Scottish border. There were also suspicious movements of French forces around the English-held towns on the French side of the Channel. It was known that many of the English living there were not altogether loyal to Mary. Indeed, the fort of Hammes was governed by Henry Dudley's brother, and many Protestants who had found life uncomfortable for them in England had settled around Calais. All these things together served to propel England into war with France without admitting that they were helping Philip by doing so.

In spite of French provocation, it still took a little time for England to come to the point of actually declaring war. At the beginning of May, Philip only had the promise of 5,000 infantry and 1,000 cavalry to aid him in the Netherlands. They were to be sent by virtue of a treaty made by Henry VIII in 1546, in which England agreed to go to the assistance of the Low Countries if they were attacked. Oddly enough, after all the hatred engendered by the Spaniards in England, both nobles and commoners enrolled gladly in Philip's service: "some from a longing for novelty, which is peculiar to this nation, some from rivalry and desire of glory, and some to obtain grace and favor with his Majesty and the Queen."[25] Philip became more optimistic. "Things are shaping well here; but they were in such a state that it has taken all this time, and will take more, to set them in order and make sure that the English will declare war without great delay. I trust there will be no weakening now in their determination, as the French make it clear what they intend to do, as witness the Stafford affair."[26]

At the end of May, Mary recalled her ambassador to the Court of Henry II, telling the French King only that she had decided to accede to her ambassador's request to return home. Mary had made the most unfortunate decision of her career. On June 7, the proclamation declaring war on France was made in London.[27] The reasons given were French support of Northumberland's treasonable plot and of the Wyatt rebellion, harboring of English rebels at the French court, acts of piracy against English ships, direct responsibility for Stafford's attack on Scarborough, unfriendly acts with a view to taking possession of Calais and the introduction of counterfeit coins into England. "For the above reasons, and because he has sent an army to invade Flanders which we are under obligation to defend, we have seen fit to proclaim to our subjects that they are to consider the King of France as a public enemy to ourselves and our nation, rather than to suffer him to continue to deceive us under color of friendship."[28] All French subjects were given forty days in which to leave the country. Philip took the declaration of war as a vote of confidence in himself. On June 9 he wrote to his ambassador in Venice, "The inhabitants of this Kingdom are proving the devotion they feel for my service, and have now proclaimed war on the King of France, as has been publicly proclaimed. This is an important event...."[29]

On the same day, the English Herald, Norroy
King of Arms, wearing a cloak of black cloth, presented
himself at the court of Henry II, who was then at Reims.
Before he could state his errand, the King interrupted
him: "Herald, I see that you have come to declare war
on me on behalf of the Queen of England. I accept the
declaration.... I forbid you on your life to speak another word. I act thus because the Queen is a woman,
for if she were not, I would employ other terms. But
you will depart and leave my Kingdom as quickly as you
can."[30] He nevertheless presented the Herald with a
chain as a sign of his generosity. The French ambassador
in London was dismissed by Mary before Henry had
time to recall him. De Noailles returned home, but on
the way lingered long enough in Calais to look round
the fortifications so that he was able to deliver a report
on their weaknesses to his master.

Henry II, in equal straits for money as the rest to
pay for the war, was also borrowing wherever he could,
"commissioners and collectors going the rounds very
diligently, nobody being let off."[31] And as a last re-
source, an inventory was drawn up of all silver objects in
the churches of France which could be melted down for
coin. The English declaration of war had been unexpected. French provocation had been intended rather to
prevent Mary from helping Philip rather than to bring
her into the war on Philip's side. "This whole Kingdom
is anxious and frightened by this declaration from the
English."[32]

There was no question that Philip would have to
leave England in order to help the defense of Flanders.
But he delayed his departure, waiting for Gomez to
return from Spain where he had been sent to raise
money and supplies. "Our fleet from Spain is delayed,"
wrote Philip to the Bishop of Arras in mid-June, "but it
seems impossible that it should not come soon, for if it

had been lost we would have heard about it....Imagine, what bad luck it would be if we were not able to begin this campaign for want of such a small sum of money, now that everything else is taking shape better than we could have wished."[33] He also said in the same letter that the Emperor had postponed abdication of the Imperial dignity until he had seen how Philip's affairs progressed. The Emperor still apparently did not have absolute faith in his son's ability to carry out his duties. The Spanish ships arrived shortly afterward. Two days later Philip left England, never to return. Mary went to Dover to see him embark and wish him well. She then returned to London, once more a lonely Queen. It was again the lot of Reginald Pole to be her chief support.

The early stages of the war proceeded as could have been expected. The English forts in France were reinforced. The French sent more troops to Scotland and the Scots made raids over the border. The English, French and Spanish ships harried each other. Frantic efforts were made by all parties to raise more money. English troops were sent into Flanders. There was excitement and even enough enthusiasm for some men to go willingly to fight, though Michiel Surian, the new Venetian ambassador, said the English people as a whole were not greatly pleased. "What weighs more with them than anything else, is to see that all this is being done for the benefit of aliens whom they detest, and most especially Spaniards. The Queen is bent on nothing else, by reason of the great love she bears her husband."[34]

The first battle was at St. Quentin in late August. The victory went to the Spaniards and the English. "Both sides fought most choicely, and the English best of all,"[35] reported one of the Spaniards (though later Mary was told, to her distress, that they had not been first to enter St. Quentin as she had believed).[36] The rejoicing in London over the victory was of the same order that greeted coronations, royal weddings and the like. Bells were rung; there were services of thanksgiving in the churches; bonfires were lighted in the streets and the populace drank its fill of wine. Mary was reported to be especially glad at the news that there had been very little loss of life, and that there seemed to be a prospect of peace between her husband and the Pope. The French, having lost the battle of St. Quentin, drew back their army from Italy, leaving the Pope to fight on alone. He became disillusioned with his French allies and was prepared to come to terms with Philip without having taken Naples from him.

Philip, not expecting the campaign to continue during the winter months, withdrew to Brussels. But disturbing news came from Calais at the new year. Lord Wentworth, the Deputy Governor, wrote to Philip on January 2 to say that he was surrounded by French troops. On January 7, the town fell to the enemy. This was a terrible blow to Mary and to the English nation and an obvious cause of rejoicing to the French. It was not clear who was to blame. No reinforcements had come to Wentworth's aid when he was beset. The English were slow to move and had not left England when they were needed. Philip's offers of help were first refused and when they were accepted, it was already too late. Wentworth and some of those defending Calais were suspected of collusion with the French, for they had surrendered after only a short bombardment; they had saved their own lives, but they had let in the enemy who had immediately taken possession of the artillery, munitions, and other supplies. Some of the Privy Council in England were also suspected of having connived with the French.[37]

Philip, although he felt that the defense of Calais had not been properly organized, had some sense of guilt, both on account of the English defeat and because

Flanders was now more vulnerable to French attack. He explained to his sister why he had been led to disband his troops prematurely. "It was then December, and there were heavy falls of rain and snow. I had no money to keep up such numbers of troops.... I regret the fall of this place more than I can express to you, and I have ample reason to do so, because it is a famous fortress and a very important one."[38] In writing to the Privy Council in England to express "his great pain and regret," he said that "it would, however, have been still bitterer to us if we felt that we had failed in any way our duty."[39]

Henry II went to inspect his regained territory and expressed surprise at the French success.[40] He said that if there had been enough soldiers to defend it or a skilled commander in charge of even a few men, Calais would not have fallen. He added that if the defenders had held out for one more day, the siege would have failed because of a terrible storm which rose up suddenly; if his troops had been outside the town instead of already within it, a great part of them would have been drowned.

Guines under Lord Grey was the next stronghold to fall. The defending forces put up a better and a longer fight than their countrymen at Calais, but in the end they too surrendered. Hammes under Edward Dudley collapsed without attempting any defense. In England there was despair and consternation. All that the war had brought them was loss of English lives, the loss of a great deal of money and the loss of the last of their highly prized possessions in France. This was not only a blow to English pride but also to English trade. No longer could they store the wool, their staple export at this time, on the continent. To store it in England would mean endless delay in sale because of the difficulties caused by the Channel crossing to buyers coming to England and the transport of wool to Europe afterward.

Philip sent Count Feria to discuss what the next moves should be and to help Mary raise more money for him as well as for herself and to raise troops to protect England from a possible French invasion. Delayed by storms, Feria arrived in London on January 27. Thereafter he reported continually to Philip on the hard time he was having in trying to fulfill his objective. The English nobles were rich but not willing to part with their riches, and the initial indignation at the French victories had soon given way to apathy. Feria wrote to Philip in March: "I am at my wits' end with these people here, as God shall be my witness, and I do not know what to do. Your Majesty must realize that from night to morning and morning to night they change everything they have decided, and it is impossible to make them see what a state they are in, although it is the worst any country has ever fallen into. If it were only a question of them, I think the best thing to do would be to let them get into the power of anyone whom might take them over, for that is what they deserve. But I am afraid they might drag us after them... The Queen tells me she is doing all she can. It is true she has spirit and goodwill. With the rest, it is hard labor."[41] He continued: "The Cardinal is a dead man, and although I have been able to warm him up a little by talking to him every day ... the result is not all I could wish."[42]

Mary from the start had tackled the problem in her usual way by prayer and action, "arranging and providing by such means as possible both divine and human, for what the present need requires, as also by ordering supplications and prayers to be made in all the religious congregations for success."[43] But her strength and her will were gradually being eroded and she no longer had any English adviser on whom she could depend. Pole, as Feria had said, was a very sick man and no longer able to cope with the problems she had to face. Her feelings toward the members of her Council had

*Mary I*

not changed. Count Feria himself, as Philip's friend and representative, became her chief support. He found consolation for his unrewarding task in England in the company of Jane Dormer, one of the Queen's ladies in waiting, whom he afterward married and took to Spain. To her biographer, Henry Clifford, we owe many anecdotes of Mary's life.

## 4. Last Days

Mary was more courageous than anticipated when the bad tidings reached England. She was buoyed up by other news which this time she had presumably waited to communicate to Philip until she was reasonably certain. On January 10, Mary sent a messenger to Philip to give him "the sure advice of her being pregnant."[44] Pole had been more cautious in his manner of conveying the information. On January 4, as the news of the fall of Calais was coming in, he wrote to Philip that the Queen was showing her usual steadfastness in times of tribulation and continued: "I was at first anxious lest such unexpected news might seriously agitate her Majesty, especially as we now hope she is pregnant."[45] Philip apparently accepted the information at its face value and said that it also helped to comfort him for the loss of Calais. "The news of the pregnancy of the Queen, my beloved wife," he wrote, "has given me greater joy than I can express to you as it is the one thing in the world I have most desired and which is of the greatest importance for the cause of religion and the welfare of our realm."[46]

A visiting Spaniard reported at the beginning of February that when he had kissed hands with the Queen, who was living in retirement as was the custom in England, he could see that she was pregnant. He said that she was expected to be delivered by the end of the month or in early March. But March came and there was no birth. Feria thought Mary was trying to convince herself that she was with child although she now knew it was not so. By the end of April, Mary had to admit that her pregnancy was just as much of a fiasco as the last one had been. Philip never mentioned it after his first formal expression of pleasure except to ask Feria to report on the health of the Queen. Whether he believed the news is doubtful, though he would have been too polite to express his doubts publicly. There is no record of how he received the information that it was again a figment of Mary's imagination. He was completely absorbed in the war which he was less and less able to afford. Mary herself, however, believed enough in her pregnant condition to make a will in March leaving her crown to the "heirs, issue and fruit of my body, according to the laws of this realm."[47]

The state of war persisted in Europe, though the fighting was gradually discontinued. Both Henry II and Philip would have preferred peace to a war which neither of them could afford, but Philip dared not agree to a truce as long as Calais remained in French hands. Having encouraged England to come into the war on his side, he could not abandon her. Mary's chief obsession was now to regain England's lost outposts in France. She struggled on, but she was dogged by illness of a more serious kind than usual. She was more prone to melancholy "and her indisposition results in business being handled more slowly than need be,"[48] wrote Feria.

Mary was still hopeful that one day Philip would return to help her in her objective but she was understanding of his absence. In May, Feria wrote to Philip, "The Queen has taken patiently your Majesty's decision not to come for the present."[49] Philip was not going to return and, even if he had wished to do so, he was far too involved in his own affairs to be able to leave home. When Feria told him that his position in England would be stronger if he paid the pensions he had promised certain members of the Council on his marriage, Philip replied that willing though he was, he just did not have the money. He also told Feria to reduce the number of people he had left behind in England, but gradually so that it would not be noticeable. The Regent Figueroa left in May ostensibly because he had another commission to fulfil for Philip in Spain. Feria himself stayed on until September. Then Mary was as alone and as sad as she had ever been in her lonely sad life.

Ill health was the lot of the principal characters in this story. Philip was the only one to recover from whatever serious ephemeral illness afflicted him in the early part of 1558. Pole was too weak to pull his weight on the Council, but he still did what he could to comfort Mary, for which Philip was grateful. "I thank you for keeping the Queen company and the devotion you show in her service, and affectionately beg you so to continue, to cheer her loneliness, for thus you are doing us the greatest pleasure."[50] Feria was not so happy about the role of the Archbishop, whose advice he did not think was always right. On September 21, Charles V died. Charles's sister, the Queen of Hungary, died eight days later, just when she was about to come back to act as Regent in Flanders again. And Mary's health deteriorated enough to become a cause of anxiety to others besides herself. Philip wrote to ask after her and sounded concerned.

Negotiations for a truce between Philip and Henry began in September, but the English were only asked to attend when matters in which they were concerned were being discussed. The meetings were drawn out and, as far as Calais was concerned, inconclusive. They were suspended and resumed on November 7, by which time it was known to everybody that Mary was dying. Again the conference was adjourned. Philip asked Feria to return to England on his behalf and to report on Mary's condition. He sent with him a Portuguese physician of great repute. But Feria was also to see Elizabeth and to ensure that the succession would pass to her and that she should marry someone acceptable to Philip. Surian, writing from Brussels, said that the rumor there was "of the King's intention to have her for himself."[51] It was important to Philip that England should continue in a friendly relationship and he believed that his kindly acts to Elizabeth in the past would ensure her cooperation in the future.

It would seem that Mary's feeling of inadequacy to deal with the ever more serious problems facing her,

her realization that Philip was not coming back, and her failure to have a child who would legitimately oust Elizabeth from the succession had aroused in her a kind of hysteria. Her former affection for Elizabeth had turned to a hatred obvious enough to have been noticed by both Renard[52] and Michiel.[53] And Philip's advocacy of kindly treatment for Elizabeth had only served to make her jealous. At first Mary had dissembled but, as she neared the end of her life, her hatred became more fixed and was given expression. She went so far as to say that Elizabeth was not the child of Henry VIII and wanted her illegitimacy confirmed and her right to the succession denied. She also felt guilty that she had not insisted on Elizabeth's marriage to the Duke of Savoy, for she feared she had lost the affection of her husband by not carrying out his express wish. Finally, Mary gave in to the pressure of her Council and consented that Elizabeth should succeed her. She asked two things of her successor: "one that she will maintain the old religion as the Queen has restored it, and the other that she will pay the Queen's debts."[54] Elizabeth did neither.

Feria arrived in England on November 7. He went to see Elizabeth as instructed but found her attitude to Philip cooler than it had been before. She was now sure of the succession and no longer needed his help. She was surrounded by courtiers ready to switch allegiance in order to secure their own positions. "In the meanwhile, the English have purchased all the cloths of silk to be found at Antwerp, and they are preparing to appear with very great pomp at the coronation of the new Queen."[55] Already the populace was ready to say *The Queen is dead, long live the Queen.*

Mary's friends rallied round her as she lay dying. She continued to find the only real solace of her life in the religious rites of her faith up to the end. Foxe reported, and the story is perhaps true because it is in character, that when her ladies asked her if she grieved for Philip's absence, she replied that it was not that alone. "When I am dead and opened, you shall find Calais lying in my heart."[56]

Mary died in her sleep on November 17, at seven o'clock in the morning in her palace of St. James. At seven in the evening of the same day, her friend and counsellor, Reginald Pole died at Lambeth. "And each departed with such piety as might have been expected from people who had led such lives."[57]

Philip was in Brussels when he heard of the deaths of his father, the Emperor, and his aunt, the Queen of Hungary. "It seems that everything is being taken from me at once. Blessed be the Lord for what he does! One must say nothing, but accept his will...."[58] Shortly afterward, while negotiating terms for peace with France (which he hoped to seal by marrying his son Don Carlos to Elizabeth the daughter of the King of France), he heard of the death of Mary. "The Calais question cannot be settled so soon, now that the Queen, my wife, is dead. May God have received her in His Glory! I felt a reasonable regret for her death. I shall miss her...."[59]

On December 14, Mary was buried in Westminster Abbey with all the rites due to a Sovereign. The Count of Feria acted as chief mourner in Philip's place. On the same day in Brussels a similar service was held. The Archbishop Pole was buried in Canterbury one day later. Dr. White, Bishop of Winchester, preached Mary's funeral sermon so eloquently and in so partisan a fashion that he was put under house arrest for a month. But what he said summarized Mary's career in the eyes of her former friends, if not in the eyes of the new Queen and her friends.

She was a King's daughter, she was a King's sister, she was a King's wife. She was a Queen, and by the same title a King also: she was sister to her, that by the like title and right, is both King and Queen at this present of this realm... What she suffered in each of these degrees before and since she came to the crown I will not chronicle... She had the love, commendation and admiration of all the world. She was never unmindful or uncareful of her promise to her realm. She used singular mercy towards offenders. She used much pity and compassion towards the poor and the oppressed. She used clemency among her nobles... She restored to the Church such ornaments as in the time of schism were taken away and spoiled. She found the realm poisoned with heresy, and purged it, and remembering herself to be a member of Christ's Church, refused to write herself *head* thereof... If angels were mortal, I would rather liken this her departure to the death of an angel, than of a mortal creature. After this sort died this gracious Queen, of whom we may justly say, *Laudavi mortuam magis quam viventem* (I have praised her more now she is dead than when she was alive)... so let us comfort ourselves in the other sister; whom God hath left, wishing her a prosperous reign, in peace and tranquility,... ever confessing that though God hath mercifully provided for them both, yet *Mariam optimam partem elegit* ([God] chose Mary for the best part) because it is still a conclusion *Laudavi mortuos magis quam viventes* (I have praised the dead more than the living)[60]

# EPILOGUE

Elizabeth ascended the throne left to her unwillingly by her half-sister, even though she had never been declared legitimate. She was acclaimed joyfully by the nobles, most of whom had secretly been on her side before and had only pretended to be upholders of Mary. The people welcomed the change for, as Mary's popularity had declined after her marriage and the burning of the Protestants, so had Elizabeth's increased. Elizabeth made no immediate move to switch the country back to Protestantism, but allowed religion to be practiced according to personal belief. Philip, sorry to lose his title of King of England and anxious to keep England's friendship, sent to ask her hand in marriage if she would vow to remain a Catholic. Much as he valued the relationship with England, he could not bring himself to marry a Protestant. Elizabeth was too wise to make Mary's mistake of choosing a foreigner for her husband. She parried the question, but indicated her willingness to remain on friendly terms with Philip.*

*England's friendship with Spain was, however, a stormy one, resulting in the outbreak of war between the two countries in 1585.

The following year Parliament passed two Acts which effectively turned England into a Protestant state once again and established the English Church in more or less the form it has today. Elizabeth did not, however, assume the title of Head of the Church. The negotiations for peace went ahead, and in April 1559 treaties were signed both between England and France and between Spain and France. Calais remained in French hands. Seven months after Mary's death, Philip sealed his treaty with France, not by marrying his fourteen-year-old son Don Carlos to the fourteen-year-old daughter of the French King, but by marrying her himself, although he was eighteen years her senior. Elizabeth pretended to be annoyed, saying that his protestations of love to her could not have been serious, though in fact she knew that Philip's wish to marry her was prompted by purely political motives.

Mary's will of March 1558, besides naming her expected child as her heir and her husband as the guardian of the child, had been full of charitable bequests to religious foundations, poor scholars, poor soldiers and other poor people. She had asked for her servants to be recompensed for their services and her debts to be paid. She also asked that the body of her mother, Katharine of Aragon, should be brought from Peterborough and that they should be buried side by side in Westminster Abbey. On October 28, when Mary knew her end was near with no child of her own to succeed her, she added a codicil asking her successor (whom she did not name) to carry out the conditions of her will. Elizabeth ignored the will, which lay unnoticed for nearly three hundred years. Katharine of Aragon remained in Peterborough. Mary was buried in Westminster Abbey, and it was Elizabeth who eventually rested by her side. At the foot of the tomb erected to Elizabeth are two small black slabs which mark the final resting place of the two sisters.

Mary's good name, which had already come to be questioned in her lifetime, was now completely lost. Elizabeth made no effort to save it from the savage attacks which were made upon it during her reign. As we have seen earlier, it was not until the nineteenth century that any attempt was made to try and see Mary as she really was.

Mary was undoubtedly a good woman, full of piety and kindliness and with the best of intentions toward her fellows. Religion was to her not just a habit, a matter of lip service or a political device, but the only true way of living. She was religious to a fault, for she could not see any other point of view about it than her own. She was behind the times, living in the religion of her mother and her forebears, with no appreciation of the revolution which was taking place in men's minds during her lifetime. (It is interesting to note that Foxe, the equally inflexible Protestant, was born in the same year as Mary.) Mary's attitude is not something for which she alone can be held responsible, for she was encouraged in her beliefs by her cousin the Emperor and his envoys, by her husband, by the older generation fanatics such as Stephen Gardiner and Reginald Pole and by the time-servers who only sought to gain preferment for themselves.

Whether by some innate weakness of character or because of the unfortunate experiences of her youth, Mary was not able to exert personal authority as her father Henry VIII had done and as her half-sister Elizabeth was to do after her. She always needed some strong-minded person upon whom she could depend to resolve the dilemmas in her own mind. When her religion did not provide the answers, first it was her mother, Katharine of Aragon, and her governess, the Countess of Salisbury, on whom she leaned. Afterward it was the Emperor's ambassador Chapuys and then Cromwell. On Cromwell's death the Emperor and his ambassadors, especially Simon Renard, became her mentors. Philip took over from them. When he left England, it was Reginald Pole, and, to a lesser extent, the Count of Feria who advised her. However, once Mary's mind had been made up for her she was not ineffective. She was generally courageous and undaunted by people or events she had to face. Her gift of oratory aided by her obvious sincerity enabled her on many occasions to silence her adversaries.

Her greatest admirers and her greatest foes have left on record their contrary opinions of her character. The angel of Pole and White was the devil of Foxe. To the Catholics she was all things good. She epitomized evil to the Protestants. Those who have read this book will, I hope, be able to make their own judgment.

# SELECTED READING LIST

## A. GENERAL

1. Read, Conyers, ed., *Bibliography of British History. Tudor Period 1485-1603*, 2nd ed., Oxford, 1959.
2. Levine, Mortimer, Comp., *Tudor England 1485-1603*, Cambridge, 1968.

## B. LETTERS AND PAPERS OF THE PERIOD

### 1516-1558

3. *Letters and papers, foreign and domestic, of the reign of Henry VIII*, ed. J.S. Brewer, J. Gairdner, R.H. Brodie, Longman's, London, 1864 -1910.
4. *Calendar of state papers, domestic, Edward VI;* Longman's, etc., London, 1856.
5. *Calendar of state papers, foreign, Edward VI*, ed. W.R. Turnbull; Longman's, London, 1861.
6. *Calendar of state papers, foreign, Mary*, ed. W.R. Turnbull; Longman's, London, 1861.
7. *Calendar of letters, despatches and state papers relating to the negotiation between England and Spain*, ed. G.A. Bergenroth, P. de Gayangos, M.A.S. Hume, Royall Tyler, H.M.S.O., London.
8. *Calendar of state papers, etc., Venice*, ed. Rawdon Brown; Longman's, London, 1881.
9. *Acts of the Privy Council*, N.S. vols. III and IV, ed. J.R. Dasent, H.M.S.O., London, 1891-1892.

## C. CHRONICLES, HISTORIES, LETTERS, ETC.
## OF THE PERIOD

10. *Antiquarian Repertory*, vols. I, II. ed. F. Grose, London, 1807, 1808.
11. *Chronicle of Queen Jane and of two years of Queen Mary*, ed. J.G. Nichols, Camden Society, 48.

12. *Commendone, The accession, coronation and marriage of Mary Tudor as related in four manuscripts of the Escorial,* translated and published by C.V. Malfatti, Barcelona, 1956.
13. *Cranmer, the remains of Thomas,* coll. by H. Jenkyns, 4 vols., Oxford, 1833.
14. *Edward VI, Chronicles and political papers,* Allen and Unwin, London, 1966.
15. *Edward VI, literary remains of* (Roxburghe Club), ed. J.G. Nichols, 2 vols., Franklin, NY., 1964.
16. Ellis, H., *Original letters illustrative of English history,* Harding, etc., London, 1825.
17. Forrest, W., *The history of Grisild the second: a narrative in verse of the divorce of Katharine of Aragon,* ed. W.D. Macray, Roxburghe Club, London, 1875. (Written during the reign of Mary.)
18. Foxe, J., *Acts and Monuments,* vols. VI and VII, ed. S.R. Cattley, Seeley and Burnside, London, 1838.
19. Halliwell, J.O., *Letters of the King of England,* 2 vols., Colburn, London, 1848.
20. Harbison, E.H., *Rival Ambassadors at the Court of Queen Mary,* Princeton, 1940.
21. Harpsfield, N., *A treatise on the pretended divorce between Henry VIII and Katharine of Aragon,* Camden Society N.S. XXI, London, 1878.
22. Leland, J., *Collectanea (de rebus Britannicis),* 2nd ed., vols IV and V, ed. J. Hearn, London, 1770.
23. Machyn, H., *Diary,* Camden Society, 42.
24. Madden, F., *Privy purse expenses of the Princess Mary December 1536 – December 1544,* Pickering, London, 1831.
25. de Noailles, *Ambassades de monsieur de Noailles en Angleterre,* ed. Vertot, Leyden, 1763.
26. "P.V." (tutor of Edward VI), *Historic narration of certain events . . . in the year of our Lord 1553,* transl. and printed by J. Ph. Berjean, London, 1867.
27. Stow, J., *Annals,* augmented by E. Howes, London, 1631.
28. *Tudor constitutional documents 1485-1603,* with commentary by J.R. Tanner, Cambridge, 1948.
29. *Tudor tracts 1532-1588,* ed. A.F. Pollard, Constable, Westminster, 1903.
30. Wood, (Green), M.A.E., *Letters of royal and illustrious ladies,* vols. II and III, Colburn, London, 1846.
31. Wriothesley, *Chronicle of England during the reigns of the Tudors,* Camden Society, N.S. 11, 20.
32. Tytler, P.F., *England under Edward VI and Mary,* Bentley, London, 1839.

## D. LATER WORKS

33. Alvarez, M.F., *Charles V,* trans. J.A. Lalaguna, Thames and Hudson, London, 1975.
34. Antony, C.M., *The Angelical Cardinal – Reginald Pole,* McDonald and Evans, London, 1909.
35. Brewer, J.S., *The reign of Henry VIII from his accession to the death of Wolsey,* 2 vols., ed. J. Gairdner, London, 1884.
36. *Cromwell, Life and Letters,* 2 vols., R.B. Merriman, Oxford, 1968.
37. Clifford, H., *Life of Jane Dormer,* ed. J. Stevenson, 1887.
38. Elton, G.R., ed., *The Reformation 1520-1559,* The New Cambridge Modern History II., Cambridge University Press paperback 1975.
39. Elton, G.R., *Reform and Reformation, England 1509-1558,* Edward Arnold, London, 1977.
40. Fuller, T., *The Church history of Britain,* Book VII, ed. J.S. Brewer, Oxford, 1845.
41. Fussner, F.S., *Tudor history and the historians,* Basic Books, New York, 1970.
42. Gairdner, J., *History of the English Church in the sixteenth century,* London, 1902.

43. Jordan, W.K., *Edward VI: The young King*, Harvard University Press, Cambridge, Mass., 1968.
44. Levine, Mortimer, *Tudor Dynastic Problems, 1460-1571*, George Allen & Unwin, London, 1973 (Harper & Row, Inc., USA, 1973).
45. *Penguin book of everyday verse: social and documentary poetry 1250-1916*, ed. D. Wright, Allen Lane, London, 1976.
46. Pollard, A.F., *Henry VIII*, Longman's, London, 1905.
47. Pollard, A.F., *Political history of England 1547-1603*, Longman's, London, 1910.
48. Pollard, A.F., *Thomas Cranmer and the English Reformation*, Putnam, London, 1926.
49. Pollard, A.F., *England under Protector Somerset*, Kegan Paul, London, 1900.
50. Powicke, M., *The Reformation in England*, Oxford, 1941.
51. Prescott, H.F.M., *Mary Tudor*, Eyre and Spottiswoode, London, 1962.
52. Prescott, W.H. and Robertson, W., *History of the reign of Charles the fifth, etc.*, Routledge, London, 1857.
53. Prescott, W.H., *History of the reign of Philip the second*, vol. I, Routledge, London, 1860.
54. Ridley, J., *Thomas Cranmer*, Oxford, 1962.
55. Scarisbricke, J.J., *Henry VIII*, Eyre and Spottiswoode, London, 1968.
56. Stone, J.M., *History of Mary I, Queen of England*, Sands, London, 1901.
57. Strickland, A., *Lives of the Queens of England*, vols. II and III, George Bell, London, 1885.
58. Strickland, A., *Lives of the bachelor Kings of England*, Simpkin Marshall, London, 1891.
59. Strype, J., *Ecclesiastical Memorials*, Vol III, ii, Oxford, 1822.
60. Tennyson, A., *Queen Mary: a drama*, H.S. King, London, 1875.
61. Watson, Foster, *Vives and the Renaissance education of women*, London, 1912.

# CHAPTER NOTES

ABBREVIATIONS (Nos. in brackets refer to Reading List)

| | | | |
|---|---|---|---|
| L. & P. | 3 | Cal. St. Papers, Edw. VI. | 5 |
| Ven. Cal. | 8 | Commendone | 12 |
| Ellis | 16 | Chronicle, Queen Jane | 11 |
| Madden | 24 | Foxe, A. & M. | 18 |
| Letters of Royal, Etc. Ladies | 30 | Tud. Const. Docs. | 28 |
| Span. Cal. | 7 | Tytler | 32 |
| Cranmer | 13 | Fuller | 40 |
| Halliwell | 19 | Prescott, Ph. II | 53 |
| Chronicle, Edw. VI | 14 | Machyn | 23 |

## CHAPTER I

1. For description of Mary's christening, see *L.&P.* II, i, p. 435
2. *Ven. Cal.,* II, p. 285
3. *Ibid.,* p. 558
4. Ellis, 1st series, I, p. 174
5. *Ven. Cal.,* IV, ii, p. 161
6. *L.&P.,* V, p. 1131
7. Henry Clifford, *The Life of Jane Dormer,* p. 80
8. Madden, Introduction, p. xlii
9. Ellis, 1st series, II, p. 19
10. *Letters of Royal, etc. Ladies,* II, p. 32
11. *Ibid.,* p. 202
12. *Ven. Cal.,* IV, p. 288
13. Madden, *Introduction,* p. liv
14. Sp.Cal. IV, 2, i, p. 527
15. The nearest extant original version of these words is to be found in *A Paris News Letter* dated seventeen days after the execution of More: "... il mourait son (i.e. the King's) bon serviteur et de Dieu premièrement." The scene at the scaffold was described some twenty years after the event by More's son-in-law William Roper and by Nicholas Harpsfield. See *The Early English Text Society,* original series, no. 186, pp. 3-6 and 266. (O.U.P. 1932.)

## CHAPTER II

1. *L.&P.,* VI, p. 491
2. *Ibid.,* p. 472
3. *Ibid.,* p. 629

4. *Ibid.,* VII, p. 31
5. *Ibid.,* V, p. 764 ('unicum et supremum dominum et quantum per legem Christi licet.")
6. *Sp. Cal.,* V, ii, p. 125
7. *Letters of Royal, etc.,* II, p. 251
8. *L.&P.,* XI, p. 7
9. Madden, *Privy Purse Expenses.*
10. *L.&P.,* XII, i, p. 227
11. *Letters of Royal, etc.,* III, p. 89
12. Cranmer, *Works,* I, p. 299
13. *Sp. Cal.,* VI, i, p. 511
14. *Ibid.,* VI, ii, p. 190

## CHAPTER III

1. *Sp. Cal.,* IX, p. 123
2. *Halliwell,* II, p. 8
3. *Loc. cit.*
4. Ellis, *1st series,* II, p. 149
5. *Letters of Royal, etc.,* III, p. 193
6. *Chronicle, Edw. VI,* p. 10
7. *Sp. Cal.,* IX, p. 419
8. *Ibid.,* p. 407
9. *Ibid.,* p. 464
10. *Ibid.,* p. 489
11. *Ibid.,* X, p. 127. (For the details of Mary's planned escape, see pp. 124-135.)
12. *Chronicle, Edw. VI,* p. 40
13. *Sp. Cal.,* X, p. 247
14. *Cal. State Papers Ed VI,* I, p. 75
15. *Loc. cit.*
16. *Ibid.,* p. 137
17. Ellis, *1st series,* p. 176
18. *Acts of the Privy Council,* N.S. III, p. 337
19. *Ibid.,* p. 351
20. *Ibid.,* p. 352
21. *Chronicle, Edw. VI,* p. 107
22. *Sp. Cal.,* XI, p. 9

## CHAPTER IV

1. *Sp. Cal.,* XI, p. 74
2. *Ibid.,* p. 81
3. Commendone, *Ms. I,* p. 16

## CHAPTER V

1. *Sp. Cal.,* XI, p. 118
2. *Ibid.,* p. 132
3. *Ibid.,* p. 156
4. *Chronicle, Queen Jane,* p. 25
5. *Sp. Cal.,* XI, p. 228
6. *Ibid.,* p. 158
7. *Ibid.,* XI, p. 314
8. *Ibid.,* p. 169

9. *Ibid.,* p. 131
10. Stow, *Annals,* p. 616
11. *Ibid.,* p. 617
12. *Sp. Cal.,* XI, p. 262
13. *Ibid.,* p. 418
14. *Ibid.,* p. 421
15. *Ibid.,* p. 247
16. *Ibid.,* p. 126
17. *Ibid.,* p. 213
18. *Ibid.,* p. 289
19. *Ibid.,* p. 280
20. *Ibid.,* p. 228
21. *Ibid.,* p. 269
22. *Loc. cit.*
23. *Ibid.,* p. 372
24. *Ibid.,* p. 363
25. *Ibid.,* p. 364
26. *Ibid.,* p. 367
27. *Chronicle, Queen Jane,* p. 36
28. Commendone, *Ms. II,* p. 67
29. Foxe, *A.&.M.,* VI, p. 414
30. *Chronicle, Queen Jane,* p. 50.
31. *Sp. Cal.,* XII, p. 125
32. *Ibid.,* p. 154
33. *Ibid.,* p. 150
34. *Ibid.,* p. 85
35. *Ibid.,* p. 15
36. *Ibid.,* p. 30
37. *Ibid.,* p. 121
38. *Letters of Royal, etc.,* III. p. 290
39. *Sp. Cal.,* XII, p. 8
40. *Ibid.,* p. 175
41. *Ibid.,* p. 185
42. *Ibid.,* p. 5
43. *Ibid.,* p. 36
44. *Ibid.,* p. 248
45. *Ibid.,* p. 295
46. *Ibid.,* p. 307
47. Commendone, *Ms. III,* p. 83. (See also Sp. Cal. XIII, pp. 7-13.)
48. *Ibid.,* p. 84
49. *Sp. Cal.,* XIII, p. 442
50. Commendone, *Ms. III,* p. 87
51. *Chronicle, Queen Jane, App.* p. 167
52. Machyn, pp. 34 and 67.
53. *Sp. Cal.,* XII, p. 322
54. *Ibid.,* p. 318

## CHAPTER VI

1. *Ven. Cal.,* VI, ii, p. 1061
2. *Ibid.,* V, p. 532, 3
3. *Ibid.,* VI, ii, p. 1064
4. *Sp. Cal.,* XIII, p. 30
5. *Loc. cit.*
6. *Ibid.,* p. 6

7. *Ibid.*, p. 26
8. *Chronicle, Queen Jane*, p. 81
9. *Sp. Cal.*, XIII, p. 33
10. *Ibid.*, p.13
11. *Ibid.*, p. 48
12. *Tud. Const. Docs.*, p. 123
13. *Sp. Cal.*, XIII, p. 60
14. Tytler, II, pp. 451- 7
15. *Ven. Cal., VI*, ii, pp. 1070-1.
16. *Tud. Const. Docs.*, p. 125
17. *Ven. Cal.*, V, p. 59
18. *Loc. cit.*
19. *Ibid.*, p. 57
20. *Tud. Const. Docs.*, pp. 95 & 124
21. Foxe, *A.&M.*, VII, p. 570
22. *Ven. Cal.*, VI, i, p. 386
23. *Register of the Martyrs in Tudor Tracts*, p. 276
24. *Sp. Cal.*, XIII, p. 139
25. *Loc. cit.*
26. *Ibid.*, p. 152
27. *Ven. Cal.*, VI, iii, p. 1647
28. Fuller, VII, pp. 236, 7
29. Prescott, *Ph. II*, I, p. 107
30. *Sp. Cal.*, XIII, p. 239
31. *Ven. Cal.*, VI, i, p. 44 (A quotation from Foxe, however).
32. *Ibid*, p. 147
33. *Ibid.*, p. 167
34. *Loc. cit.*
35. *Ibid.*, p. 174

## CHAPTER VII

1. *Sp. Cal.*, XIII, p. 248
2. *Ven. Cal.*, VI, ii, p. 1058
3. *Sp. Cal.*, XIII, p. 151
4. *Ibid.*, p. 35
5. *Sp. Cal.*, XIII, p. 247
6. *Ven. Cal.*, VI, i, p. 190
7. *Ibid.*, p. 206
8. *Sp. Cal.*, XIII, p. 250
9. *Ven. Cal.*, VI, i, p. 281
10. *Ibid.*, p. 285
11. *Sp. Cal.*, XIII, p. 207
12. *Ibid.*, p. 260
13. *Ven. Cal.*, VI, i, p. 378 sequ.
14. *Ibid.*, p. 384
15. *Ibid.*, p. 401
16. *Sp. Cal.*, XIII, p. 249
17. *Ven. Cal.*, VI, i, p. 455
18. *Ibid.*, p. 536
19. *Ibid.*, p. 434
20. *Sp. Cal.*, XIII, p. 276
21. Prescott, *Ph. II*, I, p. 120
22. *Ven. Cal.*, VI, ii, p. 1070
23. *Sp. Cal.*, XIII, p. 288

24. *Ven. Cal.,* VI, ii, p. 1095
25. *Ibid.,* p. 1086
26. *Sp. Cal.,* XIII, p. 291
27. *Ibid.,* pp. 293, 4
28. *Loc. cit.*
29. *Loc. cit.*
30. *Ibid.,* p. 295
31. *Ibid.,* p. 301
32. *Ibid.,* p. 302
33. *Ibid., p.* 297
34. *Ven. Cal.,* VI, ii, p. 1147
35. *Sp. Cal.,* XIII, p. 317
36. *Ibid.,* p. 367
37. For description of fall of Calais, see *Sp. Cal.,* XIII, pp. 337, 8
38. *Ibid.,* p.332
39. *Ibid.,* p. 310
40. *Ven. Cal.,* VI, iii, p. 1445
41. *Sp. Cal.,* XIII, p. 366
42. *Ibid.*
43. *Ven. Cal.,* VI, iii, p. 1414
44. *Ibid.,* p. 1432
45. *Ibid.,* p. 1414
46. *Sp. Cal.,* XIII, p. 340
47. Madden, *Appendix IV,* p. clxxx
48. *Sp. Cal.,* XIII, p. 378
49. *Ibid.,* p. 385
50. *Ibid.,* p. 392
51. *Ven. Cal.,* VI, iii, p. 1549
52. *Sp. Cal.,* XIII, p. 372
53. *Ven. Cal.,* VI, ii, p. 1058
54. *Sp. Cal.,* XIII, p. 438
55. *Ven. Cal.,* VI, iii, p. 1549
56. Foxe, *A.&M.,* VIII, p. 625
57. *Ven. Cal.,* VI, iii, p. 1550
58. *Sp. Cal.,* XIII, p. 440
59. *Ibid.*
60. *Fuller,* VII, pp. 246, 7

**EPILOGUE**

1. Madden, *op. cit.*

# GENEALOGICAL TABLES

## TABLE I  Mary

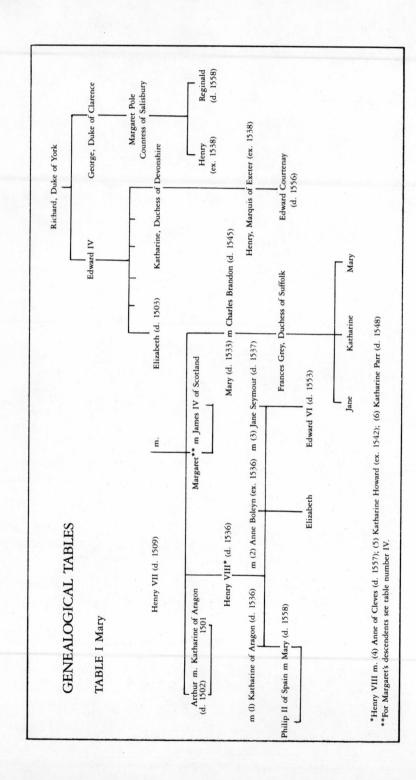

*Henry VIII m. (4) Anne of Cleves (d. 1557); (5) Katharine Howard (ex. 1542); (6) Katharine Parr (d. 1548).

**For Margaret's descendents see table number IV.

# TABLE II Philip II

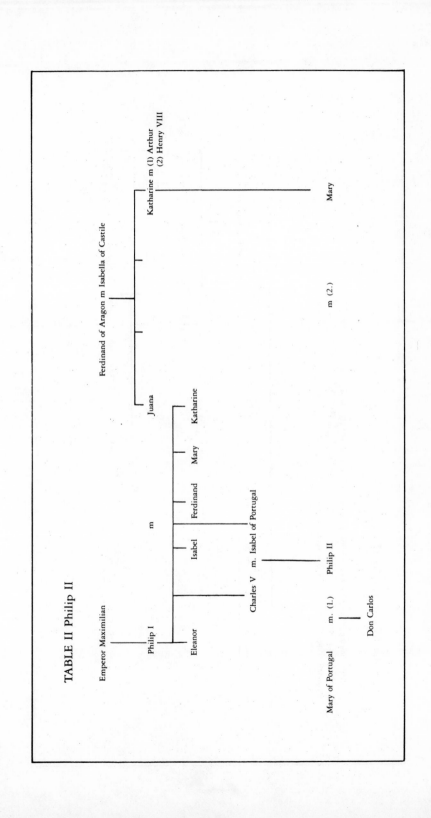

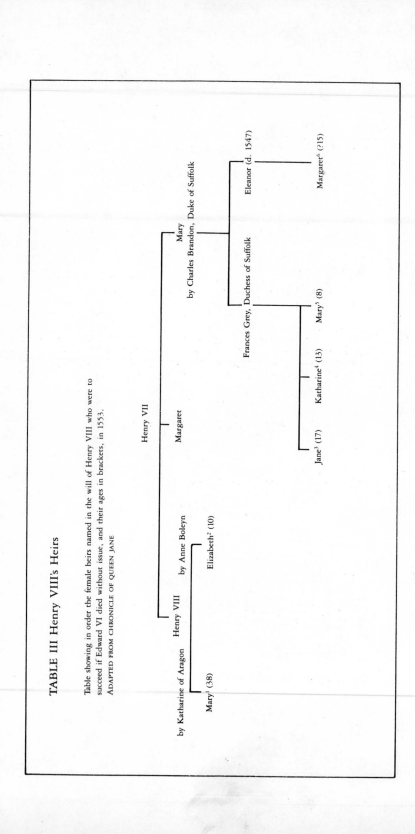

## TABLE III Henry VIII's Heirs

Table showing in order the female heirs named in the will of Henry VIII who were to succeed if Edward VI died without issue, and their ages in brackets, in 1553.
ADAPTED FROM CHRONICLE OF QUEEN JANE

Henry VII

```
Henry VIII                                    Margaret              Mary
                                                                    by Charles Brandon, Duke of Suffolk

by Katharine of Aragon   by Anne Boleyn

Mary[1] (38)             Elizabeth[2] (10)      Frances Grey, Duchess of Suffolk          Eleanor (d. 1547)

                        Jane[3] (17)   Katharine[4] (13)   Mary[5] (8)          Margaret[6] (?15)
```

## TABLE IV Margaret of Scotland

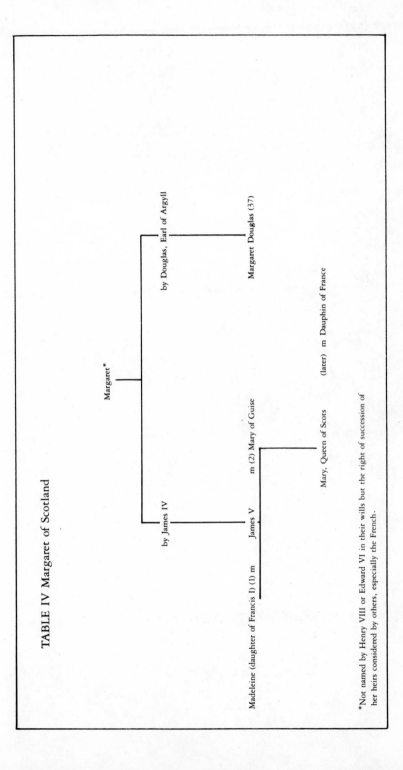

Margaret*

by James IV     James V     m (2) Mary of Guise     by Douglas, Earl of Argyll

Madeleine (daughter of Francis I) (1) m

Mary, Queen of Scots     (later)   m   Dauphin of France

Margaret Douglas (37)

*Not named by Henry VIII or Edward VI in their wills but the right of succession of her heirs considered by others, especially the French.

# INDEX

*259*